Copyright @2021 by Michael Neno

All rights reserved. No part of this book may be reproduced in any form or by any electronic or mechanical means, including information storage and retrieval systems, without permission in writing from the publisher, except by reviewers, who may quote brief passages in a review.

This publication contains the opinions and ideas of its author. It is intended to provide helpful and informative material on the subjects addressed in the publication. The author and publisher specifically disclaim all responsibility for any liability, loss or risk, personal or otherwise, which is incurred as a consequence, directly or indirectly, of the use and application of any of the contents of this book.

WORKBOOK PRESS LLC
187 E Warm Springs Rd,
Suite B285, Las Vegas, NV 89119, USA

Website:	https://workbookpress.com/
Hotline:	1-888-818-4856
Email:	admin@workbookpress.com

Ordering Information:
Quantity sales. Special discounts are available on quantity purchases by corporations, associations, and others.
For details, contact the publisher at the address above.

Library of Congress Control Number:
ISBN-13:   978-1-955459-01-3 (Paperback Version)
            978-1-955459-02-0 (Digital Version)

REV. DATE: 19/04/2021

Twisted Truth and Lies: A Sequel to the Life

By: Michael Neno

Acknowledgement

This is a way of acknowledging those who have helped me along the way.

To my loving wife Michelle, I owe you a lot since the beginning until now.

To my family and friends, you've been a big help.

Telling my story has allowed me to reflect on how far I've come to inspire more people to look always at the brighter side of life.

And also the fact that I have been supported by the very best, to whom I can only say a truly heartfelt thank you.

Introduction

Before starting the story of my life, so far, I should tell you all what I have found out and have been told about who I am and the circumstances concerning my birth and parenthood.

Also, I want to tell you that as the story is shared with you, there will be a mix of truth facts, personal belief and made up fiction. The things that I have been carrying inside for many years.

The intention being to allow to decide on what is real and what is made up BUT you may be left asking yourself questions that us normal people are not met to even know of or just enjoy a man's story.

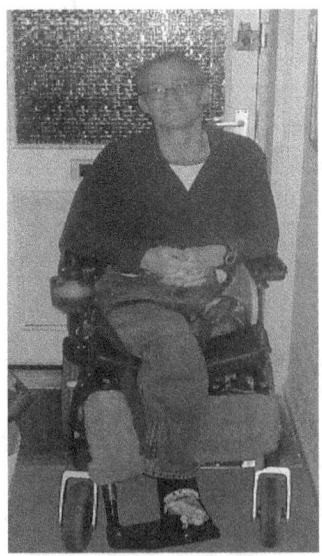

Figure 1. Home after first leg came off

CHAPTER 1

In 1964 my married mother with two children ran out on her husband and their children for unknown reasons only to become pregnant by another man who still is unknown (my father) to anybody else. After giving birth to me in 1965 she returned to her husband who took me on as one of his own. A couple of decades after her return to her husband I was told that as well as hitting herself in her stomach to cause a miss carriage she also pushed knitting needles up inside herself because she wanted to get rid of me. Since then I have proved that she has lied all along about me leaving only what others who were not involved at that time to pass on what is claimed happened because it fits their own wishes. After staying with her husband long enough to have a fourth child, my half-sister my mother ran out on all of us again when I was four years old this time for good. It was during the years after her leaving us that she became known as Ratbag to the whole family.

Coping with four children and working a full time job just to get by my dad (stepfather) must have found his life almost unbearable without the help of our next door neighbours who were great with them feeding us before going to school in the mornings. When my eldest sister who was only fifteen years old at the time failed to return home from her school we were told that she intended on joining her mother wherever she was living our family had to continue without any contact what so ever from or about her.

At that time, I must have been only a few years old and with no memory of any of it except for one instance that I can still remember which was sitting in the back seat of a car driven by my mother eating some breakfast cereal and seeing a police car stopped in-front of us. I do not know clearly remember but I have been told that my mother had abducted my step brother and I resulting in and my step father, my dad being given full parental rights for us. What I will never know is why my mother abducted me if she had already tried getting me miscarried when still carrying me in her belly

At the same time, I was informed that during the period that my mother had gone away from her husband she was living and working on Union street in Plymouth as a prostitute which may explain why my father is unknown, which I will never be able to prove mainly because she has changed her name so many times over the years while leaving no record or photographs with her in. I do know that these later times Union street is a completely different place and much nicer.

I began noticing unimportant small differences in my appearance and inclusion in things compared to my siblings mainly my hair colour with it being bright ginger compared to everyone else in the family being black and how I never led the but just follow along with whatever was going on. Even at under ten years old always. I found that when picking sides for anything in and out of school I was amongst the last to be chosen even when I had already shown myself as one of her children but tended to the better ones, something that I never let bother me. All this I tell myself means nothing and it is just my own subconscious trying to know and understand my own existence here. It was not to start to become clearer to me until about twenty years later but there is so much I believe will never be known to me and that is fine.

Coming out of my junior school aged eleven not only did I not walk just a few minutes down the road go to and get home from school any more, but I had to catch my first ever bus to travel almost three miles to the nearby town and then walk almost another mile to my new school. Knowledge and experience meant that I was slow in making new friends and girlfriends like the other children but I was happy at not being controlled and limited in everything all the time.

Moving on a while to my thirteenth birthday and ten years after my dad had remarried adding two stepbrothers to our family plus having a daughter with my new stepmother making a total of six children. With us all at school our parents were being provided for financially by dad working and mum doing the rest of the family's needs. Before leaving for work on my thirteenth birthday he sat me down and told me that he was not my real father which I had felt inside ever since being about four or five years old. Finding this out could understandably cause much upset but to me my step-parents would always be my loved parents. I just wish with all my heart that I had been a better son to them while in my teens.

Many years later I can see that I should have been. It was also at this time that I became very aware of a change in my stepmother's attitude toward me causing a sense of being rejected and a certain resentment at my even being a part of the family or even born. This I did keep to myself by not reacting badly when my year younger stepbrother started to start fights with me over nothing and blaming me when his mother broke us up and chastised me as the guilty party. She even accused me of burying my brothers new toy that I still know nothing of in our back garden.

All these insignificant little things today mean nothing to me or anyone else now and have been long forgotten with time as they should be, but at that time to me felt like I was being pushed out by my mum's side of the family because neither of my parents were blood parents to me. Luckily my half brother and sister still made a connection the family. All these little things over time I do believe played a part in my starting to make stupid choices over the next few years until I was seventeen going on eighteen years old and I so wish that I could turn the clock back and do better.

It was at the age of thirteen that I made my greatest mistake whilst playing pool with my same aged friends in one of our local pubs without any of us even thinking of booze, I foolishly played a spin on a slot machine with a coin that I had found and won more than starting with. Back then the few pounds that came out was a fortune to me being used to never having even a penny in my pocket trapping me into an addiction.

It was at this age my mid-teens that I started visiting one lad Peter who I had known and was friends with ever since first starting school and felt welcome by his parents. Although nobody really knew at that time Donna the mother often was beaten by her husband who had become a father to his lover some miles away. That I became aware of one evening as I walked into their home and found her face black and blue crying behind her very dark lens sunglasses. Instinctively I helped her to a comfy seat and made her a hot drink before sitting beside her and listening as she poured her heart to me. As she spoke I found out that she had known me since my being a baby and she had felt relatively uneasy for me after dad remarried to my stepmother.

CHAPTER 2

By the time I was 18 years old I became very aware of the true feelings at home about me when I was told how both of stepbrothers had been given an expensive wrist watch as a present but for me I never even received even a verbal happy birthday from anyone. I made up for it by paying for my own party something which I often regret as firstly I was passed out drunk before most guest had arrived and secondly my next neighbours' had brought a big box of expensive chocolates for me which had been eaten before I even saw them but really appreciated by me.

As soon as I had reached 18 years of age I transferred to working nights instead of days. This I suspect really annoyed my stepmother because she always bolted the door at night and could not on Tuesdays as this night I get home by two am. It took a very short amount of time for me to find myself locked out of my home which led me to being welcomed to stay on this night by. Donna. As she rarely slept until the early hours we would share our troubles becoming close friends. Obviously and true to form my stepmother soon started spreading rumours that I was having an affair with a married woman with kids which Donna her husband and I all knew that was untrue and finding it funny pushing both Donna and I closer together as friends. Over the course of a year I did grow to love her a lot but not romantically which several of our friends thought which I have since found out in several cases hoped would happen but I have no idea of why.

It was on one of these nights that as I reached the brow of a hill on the edge of the small village where Donna lives only a couple of minutes' walk away from my family's home that I first saw a sight that every country on the planet denies the existence of, "An Unidentified Flying Object" or UFO for short. Black and triangular in shape I watched the craft almost hovering over head of me approximately 1500 feet high with no wings and making no sound at all. Based on the decades of literature, movies and television series always portraying aliens as deadly invaders I should have been scared but I was not., I found myself wishing that they would land to say hello while at the same hoping that they would soon fly off before those in power forced or even shot it down siting national security as an excuse to take possession of alien technology that is so far more advanced than we as a species are and will remain unworthy of until we start to talk instead of Warring with each other and respecting this planet This planet that we all live on and call home by cleaning up all the pollution in our seas and the air that we breath. My eyes where transfixed by the craft for what felt like hours as a sharp beam of light from the underneath of it briefly passed over my head before shooting of away from me.

I do admit that I myself mostly believed everything that governments say in most respects but have seen the proof that the public everywhere are being lied to by the very people who do not want us knowing that in space matters humans are still nothing more than insects compared to the multitude of life forms that visit us from the stars. I also know that just as with us there are good and bad alien races and I do believe that it is a crime against humanity not to tell us all so we will know them when more come here if they are friends or dangers. This sighting was not just a one off but because I have no proof, not even a photograph I have never spoke about any of it, not even to my wife.

But that is enough of that for now so back to my story. On reaching Donna's place I wanted so much to share my experience with everyone.

My experience of that night where soon replaced by my normal life concerns like doing and being what and who everybody expected and wanted me to be. To give you an example of one such occasion when I was at Donna's home one night sharing not just her but also a couple of her best friends at the time. Archie a long-time pal of both Donna and her husband along with her best friend Joyce both took an instant liking to me which I was very thankful for. By the end of the night Joyce who is ten years my senior insisted that I went with them when Archie drove her the three miles home making it clear by her behaviour that she had decided on me as being hers.

Things at home finally came to a head one morning after returning from work when my 15year old half-sister Lorraine walked into our stepmother's anger resulting in her being knocked the width of our kitchen and hitting the washing machine hurting her causing her to cry. When I saw my stepmother raise her clenched fist about to strike another blow for crying I blocked her saying something like don't you dare hit her again or I will kill you resulting in my stepmother instantly throwing me out with just the cloths on my back. I have never regretted my action on that day but a later thing I did still does.

With nowhere to go I first went to Donna's and informed her of everything that had just happened with me which she praised me for standing up to my stepmother at last because apparently several people in the village where we lived had often expressed concern with her over different things including the dislike of me. Because Donna had to go to her work I decided to take Joyce up on her invite to visit her at home and meet her parents which after the customary welcome resulted in my falling asleep in an armchair after a long nights work previously which was understood by them. Mainly due to the circumstances my own naivety and wanting to please I just went along with Joyce and what she wanted to do.

I know now that I was a fool letting her more or less run my live away from work after she confessed to having had an affair with a married man before we met and wanting sex every time we were alone, which my being an eighteen-year-old lad who was out for sexual pleasure and experience even when visiting her friend about 20 miles away. The outcome of this at first both of us wanted to buy our own home marry and start a family, as every loving young couple. dream of doing.

In 1985 we married in church and I clearly saw my own errors in my own life and the hatred held for me by my own stepmother. In the preparation for our wedding we sent invitations to all guests with plus ones on all unmarried people but my stepmother told my two stepbrothers who we wanted as Paige boys that we did not want their girlfriends to go which was a lie, and my half-brother who I had asked to be my best man changed his mind only a few days before our big day resulting in me ask my half-sisters then boyfriend who we liked but my stepmother hated to step into the best man role. On the day the vicar told me that I had actually been christened in the same church as we were about to marry in which answered one of the countless questions that I had about myself.

As I found out later my stepmother only went to our wedding because my dad told her that if she didn't go to mine he would not go to her natural sons even though they had refused because of what their mother had told them. Although this had hurt me I received a greater blow as we were walking back down the aisle when Joyce said, "Now we are married it is your job to earn more money for what I want so I can never work again and I never want any kids" a complete turnaround on the reasons her previous wedding plans were. Who had I just committed my life wedding because my dad told her that if she didn't go to mine he would not go to her natural sons even though they had refused because of what their mother had told them. Although this had hurt me I received a greater blow as we were walking back down the aisle when Joyce said "Now we are married it is your job to earn more money for what I want so I can never work again and I never want any kids" a complete turnaround on the reasons her previous wedding plans were. Who had I just committed my life too.

At that time, I was blind to what was going on around me and was working nights for anything up to eighty, even ninety hours per week, just to keep up with my wife's extravagances. I must admit also, to avoid her family, who were at our home on most days. My wife on her part spent her day's either shopping with other members of her family or just sitting in front of the TV, watching every soap opera showing on it or so I thought until a good friend of hers told me that had seen her best friends husband going into our home very quickly after my leaving for work and leaving again only minutes before my returning home after work. Now I knew that my meant to be devoted loving wife was nothing more than a using cheating so and so.

Chapter 3

It was during this period in my life that I started to lose the feeling in my legs for short amounts of time, mostly my left one, which I was able to cope with by just getting as much rest as possible when able. I would put this down to working far too hard and stress, caused by our financial difficulties but in the late spring of 1987 my doctor, having carried out several quick tests on me in his surgery, found I no longer had any reflexes in my legs during the time that they were bad, so came to the conclusion that there was something more seriously wrong and had me admitted to hospital to undergo tests.

Originally the intended idea was to spend about three days undergoing a few tests but the three days turned into two weeks, by the end of which time all I was told was that I had got one of five medical conditions, the least serious of which was Multiple Sclerosis, so that was what would be put on my records. I was to a certain extent relieved when the doctor told me that MS was a painless condition and no one with it had ever had any kind of cancer. I am sorry to say that the doctor was totally wrong about that, as I know of people with MS having cancer and I am in constant pain myself. Fortunately for me MS is what I do have and it has turned out to be the best thing that has ever happened to me, for reasons no one could understand unless they have been in the same position.

I think the most important consequence of my hospital stay, apart from having a couple of weeks without even a visit from my wife or anyone else, was being able to see the farce that my marriage actually was and the specialist made me realize that if I failed to do anything about my circumstances, I would almost certainly find myself crippled up within twelve months. Because I could both envisage the hardships that my wife who I did still hold love for, would have to face in a future with me severely disabled and the realization that she would in no way give up, or even cut down on her extravagant life style, I left for work one night and never returned. That sounds very cold hearted of me but for several months before then I had tried my utmost to make her understand and accept that things in time were guaranteed to get worse, to no avail. At that time, I loved and wanted my wife to be free enough to find herself a new man who would be able to look after her. Selfishly on my part, I wanted to be free to date other women and play the field some before becoming disabled and becoming the one thing which I had always been uncaring about in my life I was going to become the something I had always made fun of. as a child. I have found it to be quite ironic for this to happen but now I am glad it has, for reasons that I hope will become clear as you read on. For several years I have felt as if I was being punished by God for my past and my parents' wrong doings, whatever they may have been, but now I feel I am being prepared for purposes as yet unknown to me.

With the help of a good friend and work colleague I was able to move into a small one room bed-sit flat, so as to find make a life for myself without having a wife there to put unreasonable demands on me and waste all of the money I earned. My hope is that my tale will introduce you to the feelings and emotions that do exist within disabled people, that a lot of society still refuse to accept and unfortunately, in a lot of cases do not recognize the existence of especially disabilities that are not visible. Because of the financial difficulties that I took with me on leaving Joyce, the next eighteen months were consumed by working every hour that I could, just to enable me to pay off the debts that had accumulated during my time with her and with each commitments being settled, I found myself slowly able to go out and socialize again.

For the seven years taken to divorce I worked hard and played hard getting as much out of life as I could before the inevitable disability got me along with the painful muscle spasms shooting what felt like bolts of electricity up through both of my legs. I found myself becoming quite the rebel by buying myself a 100cc motorbike. It also included buying expensive goods, and having countless girlfriends including getting engaged once, only to be dumped as soon as I informed the girl of my medical condition. Eventually things did take a turn for the better when I landed myself a new job working days rather than nights doing less hours for more money than I had been getting, plus I purchased and moved into a small place of my own the very place that my ex-girlfriend and I looked at to buy together. On top of all this, I met Sharon whilst shopping at a local supermarket, very easily falling in love with her, something that I had promised myself not to do again after being put through so much hurt in the past.

Sharon was a petite woman about five feet six inches tall, shoulder length mousy blonde hair, brown eyes and a smile warm enough to melt even the coldest of hearts, all set within a beautifully framed body. At first we just stopped and chatted whilst shopping, as a couple of friendly strangers would do but very soon we were meeting up and going out together mostly only for a hot drink at a local cafe. As our relationship blossomed it became clear to us both that sooner or later we would find ourselves in bed together and inevitably that was exactly what we quickly found happening.

It happened on a very cold and wet Friday evening in mid-October when we met up together whilst doing our weekly shopping. Outside of the supermarket the wind was howling so strongly that the small sapling trees planted around the car park were almost being uprooted from the ground and the drains were over flowing from the torrential rain pouring down from the thick, dark clouds overhead. After we had paid for our goods I asked Sharon if she would like to go somewhere and have a drink as in a coffee, to which she answered, "Yeah, okay. My place is too far away so let's go back to yours and you can make us a cup of coffee." I was surprised by this answer but still I said OK.

Arriving at my home we were both cold and soaked through, so I did the gentlemanly thing and took Sharon's wet coat from her, hanging it over my central heating radiator to dry, then brought her a clean towel to dry her hair with. I remember the way she tossed her head back so as to get her hair away from her face, before handing it back the towel and thanking me for being so nice and considerate to her. I must have gone red in the face or something because Sharon, who seemed to know exactly what was going through my mind, looked at me very seductively and said, "I know we aren't dating or anything like that but the rain has soaked right through my clothes to my skin, so can you let me borrow something to put on if I undress, to let my clothes dry?"

Even I with my shyness could tell that there was another reason for her wanting to undress other than her clothes being too wet, so I said, "If you want I've got a full length dressing gown that you're welcome to put on. I'll just get it for you." I left Sharon in the lounge and went to my bedroom for the gown, returning to find her standing totally naked before sitting on my couch. I handed her the gown, trying my hardest and not very successfully, to notice her pert rounded breasts or her beautifully shaped hour glass figure but that did not bother her at all and instead of being embarrassed she stood up and started to undress me because, as she noted, I was myself soaked through to the skin. I will not go into what happened on that day and leave it to you to imagine for yourself.

Over the course of the weekend together, I was able to tell Sharon as much about my illness as I could, which amounted to very little. I told her of my family, who had as good as killed me off by telling people that I had died of AIDS passed on by my natural father who nobody knows of and my everyday life in general. When Sharon talked about herself and her family it was with a certain amount of distress and a lot of hurt because of something that had happened to her as a teenager at home. I told her that she need not talk about it if it was upsetting to her but she just said, "You didn't have to tell me about your illness and what your family did to you so I want to tell you about myself. You are lucky because how many healthy people now will become disabled or even die as they grow older and not know it."

She carried on, "I went out with one guy at school who used to get me drunk so he could have sex with me. The bastard got me pregnant and done a runner. My mom and dad kicked me out and disowned me after making me have an abortion. Now they always try splitting me up from my boyfriends because they have a high status and powerful friends to protect. Don't take this wrong but if we are going to get together I want it to be our secret." A secret love suited me fine, as my own family disapproved of me even thinking of having a relationship because I was going to be a cripple as they called it and the idea of having one in the family was unthinkable. So there we were, two people rejected by our own families and all alone, thrown together by circumstance. How could I possibly of known that everything she said and done was all one big cruel invention by her which with time I would discover in a life shattering way.

With so many things I believed in common it was inevitable that Sharon and I very quickly became more than either of us had envisaged at the start or at least me, when all we ever did was speak to each other whilst shopping and by the end of 1992, our romance had developed into something greater, with Sharon becoming pregnant over the Christmas but as always when things were going good for me, circumstances threw a spanner in the works.

It was at the start of May when, whilst working, my legs kept giving out from under me, giving me intense pain and a semi-permanent limp. I forced myself to carry on working and made myself do more but eventually I was forced to visit the doctor, who straight away signed me off work until such time as my legs were OK enough to return but that would never happen for me. Within a matter of a few weeks I found myself in a wheelchair and unable to even leave my home, due to a very steep slope outside of my front door. Well, that is not exactly true as I could get out but there was no way that I could possibly get back in without help. At that time, it was just as well being like that, as for a short time although I had accepted my illness, I constantly asked myself why me and not someone else? Due to her claimed work as a secretary for a local solicitors' office, Sharon was unable to see that much of me, leaving the social services to pick up the pieces and find a way to help me with everything from housework to shopping.

In order to assess my daily needs I was appointed a qualified social worker to let me know how my life would be affected by being disabled. On her first visit this 'so called' professional took no time in telling me that as a cripple, or to be politically correct, a disabled person, I was no longer allowed to even think of dating and relationships, let alone fathering a child but I already had a girlfriend who was half way through a pregnancy, so because of her mannerism I failed to mention it. Over the next few weeks all I got was, "You can't do this, you can't do that." It seemed and felt as though the very system that was meant to help, was in a way segregating me from the rest of society and for the very first time, my eyes were opened to my own past cruel and cold hearted attitude toward disabled people that I had been guilty of myself in the past and I can honestly say that I was ashamed of myself. Although for a while it was only my legs that no longer work, the very fact that I eventually had no choice but to use a wheelchair gets the response from a part of sociability in general that I must be deaf, stupid, useless and in some way mentally retarded, even crossing the road to avoid talking to a disabled person. After receiving so many negative responses from every direction, I very foolishly came to the conclusion that I had to turn away from Sharon and our as yet unborn child, to give them the opportunity of finding a better life with someone else. The hardest thing was having to tell Sharon everything that I had been told and the subsequent decision stupidly made by me.

It was a warm and sunny night in mid-June as we lay beside each other in bed that Sharon turned to me saying, " What's up? I can tell there is something troubling you. Tell me what it is, I may be able to help you out." With that, struggling to find the right words I told her everything that I had been told by the social worker and my decision. She was understandably upset by this but reluctantly agreed with me, telling me that even splitting up she would still let me see our child and bring it to see me as often as she could. At that time, I sincerely believed that I was doing the right thing for all concerned bearing in mind the countless horror stories we have all heard about the social services and their immorally taking new born babies with lies and untruths to adopt out for the money paid to them by the government, but I was still able to be there with Sharon when on the 29th September 1993, our child was born, a girl who we agreed on calling Kelly after her grandmother.

Over the following month, with my help Sharon. became reunited with her family as she claimed they were and moved away, taking Kelly with her so as to be closer to them. On the first Sunday of November, Sharon's father collected her and Kelly to take them back to her parent's home in the north of London, promising to never stop his daughter from seeing me. With a face awash with tears, we had one last kiss farewell whilst swearing to keep in touch and spend holidays at my place, so that I could still see my daughter. She kept her word and whatever Kelly needed I made sure she received it, be it clothes or toys and anything Sharon, as her mother needed for her, she also got which suited her. And what did I get, well I got to see and know that my daughter and her mother were needing for nothing, whilst at the same time I was able to see them both by them visiting me. These visits gave me the courage and incentive I needed to fight against my illness and the prejudices that were destroying my life but as so often in the past, in the April of "1995" I received even more bad news. This time the news that I received got me so depressed that it brought me to the edge of being suicidal.

On Monday the 16th April 1995 I received the telephone call that all parents fear above all things, informing me that three days earlier on Friday the 13th, also Good Friday, Kelly had died in her sleep at just over 18 months old and nobody had even had the decency to call me until the Monday afternoon. On hearing this news, the mug of coffee that I was drinking went smashing onto the floor, sending splinters of china flying in every direction and I broke down and cried out aloud bursting into tears, surprising the two local teenage children who were visiting me at the time.

One of the children, a 13-year-old girl called Marree became very upset at the sight of me crying, having only ever seen me happy and smiling, whilst the other child, a 15-year-old boy called Josh, could tell that I had received bad news got to his feet and said, "I think we had better leave now Marie because I think that Mike needs some time alone." He then turned to me saying, "I'll let my sister know so you can talk to her if you want." I already knew Josh's sister, 17-year-old Stephanie, from her regular evenings at my place watching videos and just chatting about anything, so I knew that if I was ever going to talk about my daughter to anyone she would be the easiest and most understanding to open up to having been there for her brother in the past. What made everything that much harder was the fact that no one even knew of Kelly because Sharon and I had decided to keep our relationship secret and hidden from everyone else right at the start of our relationship with each other. At her request when we first met. I only spoke to a couple of trusted friends but to everyone else I had to be the same person as before.

All in all, I had to carry the pain of losing my daughter inside me for over a year, with only a very select few having the slightest idea of what had happened because neither Sharon nor I had let it be widely known and how can you talk about your child's death when no one knows you even had one. Our secrecy had in a way backfired on me. Things had been a little easier for Sharon as she was the one who had the baby with her, whereas I never even had a photograph of my child, meaning that to everyone around me I was just a single disabled man in a wheelchair. After being taken to Kelly's funeral by a friend, of Sharon she moved away from home again moving I was told to Scotland, where I lost all contact with her. It feels strange to admit now but in our time together, she never even told me her sir name and I never thought to ask.

Chapter 4

Again I found myself living alone and the subject of other people's pity and unjustified ridicule, just as I had been in the past, so although I found it very patronizing being on the receiving end of it, I accepted it and even was made able to make fun out of myself. I was still in my own home, be it what it was, a small two room flat and apart from a home help visitor for a few hours per week and regular visits from a couple of local children, I was as good as shut away, unable to even get in or out of my home not because of my disability but because of the steep slope outside of my only door to the outside world.

After several months of living like this, a well-meaning care worker suggested joining different social clubs to enable me to meet new people. Something I was open to but I very quickly discovered that being disabled mostly restricted me to clubs designed wholly for disabled people, where for one morning or afternoon a week I could sit in a room surrounded by other disabled people like myself and talk about our problems. For me to be surrounded only by other disabled persons only reminded me of my own problems and I was already well aware of them, so I declined the idea. I needed no reminder of the difficulties that being disabled, as I had to face them every day of my life.

What I wanted more than anything was to be looked at for me a man who couldn't walk, not looked at as a wheelchair with just another cripple in as unfortunately I have been many times over the years. I wanted to go where I wanted and when I wanted, without having to have a carer or social worker with me taking control and making decisions for myself. I may have been disabled but I was still a man with the same wants and desires as every man has, but to the rest of society, the politicians and the system in general, there was still an unofficial Dickensian way of thinking about the disabled. This situation plus the lack of a cure, or even an effective treatment, stood in the way of me finding a good woman to spend the rest of my life with. How was I to know that what I believed was love was only a few years, a lot of let downs and many miles, away from me. It was at this time and during a regular visit to the specialist who had originally diagnosed my condition, that an offer was made for me to spend two weeks receiving treatment in a specialist rehabilitation unit in the grounds of a large hospital, plus it was in a city that I had only visited once as a child and where I had been diagnosed so I straight away accepted it. I returned home again thinking that maybe now I would actually get the help that I not only wanted but in a certain way needed. Straight away I started sorting out the things that I would need to take with me like clothing, personal care things and of course, something to keep my mind busy between treatments. This included a couple of books to read and a personal cassette player with a few music tapes. A few weeks later at nine o'clock on a Monday morning an ambulance arrived to take me to the rehab centre and eager to go I was already down at the bottom of the slope outside of my door waiting.

On arriving at the centre I was first struck by its wheelchair accessibility and its surprisingly quiet position away from the main hospital. The building itself was a large, red brick structure, with large windows to the right of some double doors, at the top of a gentle slope, easy for getting up and down in a wheelchair when alone. Going in through the open doors I noticed a small seating area with comfy armchairs along one wall, facing a large TV and a centrally placed coffee table. "You must be Mike? I'm your named personal nurse. You can call me Emma and I'll be getting you settled in today." came a voice from in front of me. I looked up and saw my named nurse standing about five feet away from me, a good six feet tall, about her mid forty's, slim with short cut, brown hair, spectacles and a warm friendly smile.

With the introductions over, Emma took me along the carpeted corridor to the room that I would be calling home for the next two weeks. Putting my bags onto the bed Emma pointed out the toilet, bathroom and emergency alarm bell, in case I needed help at any time during my stay, before leaving to get my folder file to take some notes for their records. Beside my bed was a wardrobe and chest of draws so I started to unpack my bags, with Emma returning before I could finish. It did not take long to get the necessary forms filled out and once done she gave me have a timetable for the week's program.

Every day was set out the same starting with breakfast at 8.30am, then the day would go like this:

From 9am until 10 I was booked for physiotherapy

    A coffee break at 10.30 then nothing until lunch at noon

    From 1.30 pm until 2.30 I had more physiotherapy

    At 3 pm coffee break

    At 3.30 pm until 4.30 I was given Occupational Therapy

    Finishing off with evening meal at 5.30 pm

This routine was set for Monday until Friday, leaving me the weekend with nothing to do. The patient's physical welfare was not the only thing that the staff was interested in because before the end of my first afternoon, I was also offered the services of a councillor and a spiritual adviser, which I politely declined.

One thing that Emma asked me which quickly brought on a blush was did I need help dressing and help with my personal hygiene, meaning bathing, shaving and going to the toilet, all things I instantly said no to. I was able to bring a smile to her face when jokingly I asked if I could have a bedtime story.

By the time I left the rehab centre the following Friday, I had not only found out that not only was I born in the hospital but my mother had been on the very same ward as I had been diagnosed. I kept a promise that I had made to myself on the first morning, in that although I entered in a wheelchair I would leave on my feet be it freely or on crutches.

Getting home again I had to readjust myself to the cramped quarters and the slope that even on crutches was beyond my physical capability to get up on my own. Another thing hard for me was the non-existence of any follow up Physio, nor use of any equipment required to do it myself, leading me to have a relapse and finding myself back in a wheelchair within three weeks. This routine of spending two weeks getting help, improving, only to be followed by a relapse, happened three times for me during the next two years until I finally said not again.

It was another Friday the 13th that with only 48 hours' notice I was able to move into a specially adapted bungalow in a nearby village, to start a whole new life for myself. Over the following few years that I had to wait to find my true love, my life changed an awful lot starting only four weeks after moving into my new home. It happened when an old friend who had been working in Europe for several years returned to England and got back in touch after hearing of my disability.

Rob, a big built muscled man and about my own age sprung a surprise visit on me by just turning up on his motorbike, out of the blue one Wednesday afternoon in early December, to inform me that he and his friends, also bikers, had decided that they were not going to let me rot away feeling sorry for myself and go through Christmas and New Year shut away and all alone. Unbeknownst to me Rob, who had been my Best Man when I had got married, had arranged for me to be taken out to the parties and get-tether's that I had been so used to frequenting before my legs packed up, working with the help of some biker friends of his. He only stayed for a couple of hours but in that time arrangements were made for the forthcoming weekend, as a trial run for the quickly approaching festive time.

The Friday afternoon arrived and the usual quiet that surrounded my new home was shattered by the sounds of bike engines being revved up outside of my kitchen window. It was Rob accompanied by two other motorbikes and a Trike driven by a cuddly yet full figured woman. I was so captivated by her enchantingly full-of-life character and sense of humour, that I failed to notice the folded up wheelchair positioned at the side of her. It was Rob who, on noticing the instant attraction, introduced me to Katherine, a 25-year-old girl and ex-biker who, after a bad accident a couple of years previously, had lost the bottom of one leg. With the help of a charity for disabled bikers she had got herself mobile again by having her Trike, a three wheeled machine, a mixture of both car and motorbike, built and adapted for her. After some quick introductions to everyone Rob stood ready to help me, as I clambered up and onto the back seat of Katharine's Trike before folding up my wheelchair and strapping it beside me on the back and before long we were on our way.

After driving for about thirty miles through the often narrow country lanes we pulled into the car park of an out-of-town restaurant public house where the proprietor, who's own child was disabled, had adapted the establishment to enable good wheelchair access with proper disabled toilet facilities for the disabled customers.

Once parked up Rob got my wheelchair ready for me to get back into then Katherine, walking on a newly received false limb that very morning, then pushed me onto and up the gentle slope to the doorway and over to a table close to the bar. Leaving us there Rob went to the bar, returning quickly with a tray of drinks for everyone at the table. With Katherine already to my right Rob whispered in my left ear, "I think she likes you. Maybe you should get together." to which, taking a quick look in her direction, I replied with, "Nah she's far too good looking to be interested in me." "I wouldn't be so sure of that." came a whisper in my other ear from Katherine, accompanied with a gentle kiss on my cheek. I was to say the least surprised by this, as I had only had dirty, disapproving and disappointed looks from women up until then and to be honest, my initial thoughts were that Rob and Katherine must be poking fun at me.

By 9.30pm the place was filling up with the general public, with music playing and a lot of laughing and joking I was able to relax and join in with the fun and games. Something that did surprise me was the way that no-one at my table had a single alcoholic drink all night, so when we left we were all still sober, something not expected from a group of bikers.

On leaving we all went our separate ways, with Katherine having the job of taking me home again, where I myself managed to get my wheelchair off of her Trike and opened for me to get into, without any help. After having an unexpected surprisingly long kiss, I expressed my thanks to her for a lovely night out and she asked if she could come and visit me again because she considered me to be really nice. Saying yes, I did wonder if she would have said that if she had known what I was thinking as we kissed goodnight to each other. As I watched her pulling away on her machine I honestly did not expect to see her again, unless it was at a party with Rob and his biker friends but as it happened, I was to be proved quite wrong and I am glad that I was.

At 10.30 the following morning I was distracted from what I was doing by the sound of Katherine pulling up outside. To say that I was glad to have her come back would be an understatement to say the least but she was and she was alone. On hearing my doorbell ring, I pushed a button on the remote control device I had that automatically opens the door and in she came. Dressed in a pair of tight leather trousers, a waist length, white lace top under a leather bike jacket with tassels dangling from the sleeves and her long curly black hair, hung hair over her shoulders, she was looking the picture of beauty to me. "You did say that I could come back last night so here I am. Now just one question........Are you going to put the kettle on and make me a drink or what?" Straight away I went into the kitchen and made us both coffee, returning with her drink carefully positioned between my legs, so as to enable me to have both hands free for moving my wheelchair, before returning to the kitchen for my own drink. Once back in the lounge with Katherine I very quickly noticed that she had taken off her jacket and the flimsy lace top that was under it hugged her figure, emphasizing her large, ample, yet firm breasts.

We talked and talked about the previous night, her Trike, and our disabilities for hours before Katherine turned to face me and looking straight into my eyes said, "We've been here just talking for hours now and after last night you haven't once tried coming on to me. Are you gay or something or maybe you're afraid of me, or yourself because we're disabled and society thinks we're broken and useless, because if you are I'm going to leave right now." Hearing that from another disabled person justified my own thoughts about the people around me. With that she gave a little smile before continuing with, "I know you're not because Rob's told me that you've been married before. It's just that normally guys only want me for one thing and I'm sick of being used like a piece of sex fun then thrown away by others, who think that coz I've lost part of my leg I must be desperate and I'll do anything." I replied with, "You're lucky, I only get, you're a cripple so you're not able to give me what I want to satisfy me." It very quickly became obvious that for both of us, being disabled had changed other people's perspective of us, to no longer being people but just cripples, who do not actually matter anymore. "Well, how come you haven't tried it on with me yet? After kissing you goodnight last night, I was sure you fancied me. Was I wrong?" came her next comment to which I responded with, "After the sort of shit I've been put through by girls in the past I never ever make the first move. "With that she leaned over me and kissing me on the lips said, "So I'm making the first move on you now, OK?" That was the signal for me to respond and become more personal. Before Katherine left that night, we had become boyfriend and girlfriend.

All over that festive season Katherine and I were hardly ever being apart from each other's side. I remember Christmas Eve in particular, when the two of us visited the local Tesco store to buy some food and drink for the following day and the fun we had before facing and fighting our way through the bustling crowds of shoppers, all rushing to get their last minute supplies before the store closed. As we went along the fresh meats section, we were able to witness the store security guard trying to separate a couple of elderly woman fighting over the last fresh turkey, watched by loads of other shoppers. The sight of these two old ladies, barely five feet high, bashing each other with their handbags had everyone rolling around in fits of laughter. What made this more enjoyable was the way that, as they fought over the turkey, Katherine was able to take it for us. Seen by a member of staff we were whisked away, to avoid any repercussions off anyone else.

With Christmas Day and Boxing Day over, Rob, very aware of our involvement and knowing that Katherine had as good as moved in and was living with me, visited to invite us to a New Year's Eve party being held at the same establishment as our first night out. Obviously we accepted and a few days later, on the night in question, we were partying like animals along with everyone else. Not caring about what others thought, Katherine wore a very short skirt over a pair of black leggings below a quite revealing lace top with no bra underneath, practically showing to every guy and gal her breasts, which she was proud of. Several times she was approached by a man who she instantly rejected and pushed away, only to kiss and hold me. At one point Rob who with his latest girlfriend, almost got into a fight with another man for saying that we were how it should be, cripple with a cripple and not a cripple with a normal person. On the stroke of midnight both Katherine and I declared our love to each other, sealing it with a very long passionate kiss.

The one thing, that in a way made me realize that our relationship would not last forever, was the way that Katherine wanted to have sex in more and more in unusual places or so I thought at the time.

Looking back, I think the special connection between Katherine and I was in the way that with both of us being disabled, enabled us to laugh and joke at, and with each other, without being offensive or degrading. I was able to call her my little stumpy, while she in turn called me her own meat on wheels, without causing any upset, something which often annoyed Kath when able bodied people called her the same things as I did. For several months we had a very loving relationship together and to a certain extent some of the best sex that I ever had but in time we drifted apart and moved on.

During this time, I made a discovery that upset and hurt me inside more than anything While out one day I came upon Rob who told me that both of my grandparents had passed away within five days of each other eighteen months earlier and not one member in my family had told me I know that it had been about a decade since last seeing them, but I had never even suspected any of the resentment that the family carried for me. With them passed I made a conscious decision that if that was what they wanted I would be to them as well as doing something good despite my disability to honour my grandparents' memory as well as that of my daughter.

Chapter 5

During my time with Katherine I was able to find the courage to have my own Trike specially built and adapted, so that I could become independent again. This was something I have often regretted for various reasons, whilst at the same time I can no longer imagine my life without it.

Taking about six months to build to the right specifications I was, as you can imagine, like a child on their birthday or a young man losing his virginity, the day I was informed that my Trike was finished. An added bonus was the news that a national biker magazine was going to do an interview and take pictures with a topless model. It was disappointing when I first did the interview and had some photos taken but due to it being cold and wet, the model hoped for, never came.

Very soon that was forgotten about until I received an unexpected phone call at home. I had already spent a couple of weeks doing interviews for magazines, newspapers and television when on a Monday night in November "97", my telephone rang and on answering it I found myself talking to a woman I was later to discover, as being a nude model and soft porn actress called Zandra. She told me that whilst chatting with a topless model friend, she had been told about this wheelchair-bound biker and his three wheeled machine, that she was supposed to have photos taken with. She went on to say that her friend had made up an excuse to get out of it because being photographed with a cripple may have affected her career.

Zandra then went on tell me how, feeling sorry for me, she had done some checking up and would like to meet me sometime. Just like most other men I straight away agreed to meet her. I do not know what information she saw on me but two days later on the Wednesday lunchtime I found myself in the local town centre, waiting for her to meet me. Although the weather was overcast, it was dry and not cold at all, when a young woman with long, wavy, blonde hair, dressed in skin tight jeans, baggy jumper, knee-length boots and a quilted, red jacket, sporting a bag over her right shoulder, walked straight up to me and after asking if I was Mike, and introduced herself to me as Zandra. I personally never saw anything particularly stunning in the woman before me with the exception of her eyes, which were as men describe as sexy come-to-bed ones.

Within five minutes she asked if we could have sex, which I straight away turned down, saying that I would be pleased to have a coffee and chat but because neither of us knew anything about the other, that was as far as I would go because I still had high morals and ethics. Surprised by my answer she said, "I'm very sorry if my talk has upset you it's just that being in the sort of work I'm doing it's expected from me. I don't especially like it but I've had to get used to it." I could not help but feel a little sorry for her and I assured her that firstly I was not upset and in a way, I was honoured by the thought. With our minds put at ease we found it very easy to talk and by the time that I left her, about an hour and a half later, I had agreed to see her again but as a friend only. Zandra was happy with that and promised to call me in a day or two to arrange to see me again, to which I was happy to do.

Not expecting to hear from her again it came as a big surprise, when a week and a half later my telephone rang and she was on the other end. Picking up the phone I was greeted with, "Remember me? I said that I'd call to arrange to see you again, so here I am. When would you like to see me, or should I ask if I can see you again?" Getting over my initial surprise I said, "Yes you can see me again." I paused for a second or two before adding, "For a coffee again or maybe to go out for a meal." I have no idea why I mentioned going out for a meal because I was skint and could only afford a cheap one with no extras. Luckily for me she came back with, "A meal sounds nice but it's my treat because if we get on as well as the last time that I saw you, I might want to make a confession soon after." I was intrigued by this comment of hers and very quickly arrangements were made to meet the following Saturday.

When Saturday arrived I met Zandra mid-afternoon at the same place as our first meeting, where she asked if she could get changed for going out at my place, which I agreed to but first I would have to take her back home on my Trike. Zandra was a little hesitant on first seeing it but once we set off she soon started to love it. As I drove back to my place (the long way), I could see her face in my wing mirror and her long hair blowing back in the wind. Reaching my place, she likened being behind me on the Trike to being on a fair ground ride, which pleased me immensely. Once indoors I called a local restaurant and booked us a table, making sure that they knew there would be one person in a wheelchair. It was decided that, so we could get ourselves ready, I should use the bathroom while Zandra made us a cup of coffee and get her clothes sorted out from the small case that she had brought with her.

Putting Zandras bag in my bedroom she noticed that it was en-suite to the bathroom and had a door to the lounge. Waiting for the sound of me getting into the bath, she entered with a drink, offering to wash my back for me. Once my initial embarrassment at being seen naked by her had subsided, I tried turning the tables on her by saying, "I only let a person bathe me if firstly, they're a woman, secondly they're single and thirdly, they're in the water, as naked as I am." I should not have said that because she disappeared for a couple of minutes, only to return stripped naked and climbed into the bath with me. Under different circumstances things could have got quite rude but I kept things under control by getting out and leaving her there. After she had finished and got out she said, "Did I say or do the wrong thing just now. If I did I am very, very sorry." Seeing that she was a little unsure I settled her down by saying, "I'm not annoyed at you, I was just thinking that if we had started getting dirty we wouldn't have had time to eat for a couple of hours." "I hope that's the only reason." came her reply, to which I said it was, hiding my own feelings of here we go again, another user. I had finished dressing in into a two-piece suit, with a silk shirt, whilst Zandra was in the bath, so I left her to finish getting herself ready and entered the lounge to wait. When she finally joined me in the lounge she looked beautiful in a black, thigh-length, satin, evening dress with matching high-heeled shoes and her hair put up like it had been done professionally. She told me that even being in a wheelchair, I was looking handsome and I told her that she indeed looked beautiful. Obviously, dressed as we were, using my Trike would be a mistake and so I called a taxi to pick us up.

Entering the restaurant about half of a mile away called, "The Hare and Hounds" I felt very proud to be escorting such a beautiful woman out for a meal, this was indeed a special night for me. I remember thinking how all of the men, watching with their tongues hanging out, must be asking why it was a cripple like me with this woman and not them, but Zandra could not do enough for me and ignored everyone else. The restaurant had a split-level eating area decorated in an old world style, with oak pillars and beams sporting several hanging baskets, holding a variety of vines. Tucked away in the corners and alcoves were tables designed for two, which had vases holding candles, placed centrally. It was in one of these quiet corners where Zandra and I sat for our meal of sirloin steak, side salad and champagne to wash it down with, the champagne being Zandra's choice.

While eating a desert of fresh fruit salad and ice cream, I became aware that her eyes were not leaving me and looking at her the look in her eyes, was like she was looking for answers to questions I had no idea of, so I asked her about the confession that she had hinted at making to me on the phone, to which she just said, "Later." and changed the subject. I took the hint that this was not the right time or place for her to share her secret and did not mention it again but much later that night I was to get the surprise of my life, which you can guarantee caused a lot of hurt to me.

After having and sharing such a lovely night out together we returned to my place, where Zandra hesitantly asked me, in the sweetest tone of voices, if I would mind her sleeping over that night, as she did not have to return home until the following night and she wanted to spend some more time with me as I treated her like a lady and not a sex object. Before agreeing to letting her stay, I had to make sure she understood that by staying, it would only be as a friend. Only having the one bedroom I delegated myself to the couch in the lounge and gave up my bed to her for the night.

The next morning over breakfast Zandra asked me to let her visit again, so I told her that would be OK as long as she realised that in doing so, it would have to be as a friend only, to which she agreed. Once finished with our breakfast I took her out for another ride on my Trike before taking her to the train station for her to return home. Saying goodbye to me she said, "Thank you ever so much for last night, you made me feel like a real lady and you acted like a real gentleman. You are so nice that I never even notice your wheelchair when I'm with you." I returned her compliment with, "Thank you. Being in the company of you I'm not even bothered by your choice of profession." and kissed her gently on the lips. Before climbing onto the train we once again agreed on another visit the following week, when she again asked if she could stay over, which because the previous night had gone smoothly I agreed to.

With Zandra gone I thought very little about it, except the confession never made and the question of why she would wish to see me again because after all, I was just a cripple struggling to survive on the small government hand out that I received each week. No, saying that it was just a small hand out is probably a bit unfair. I was given enough to buy my food and pay the bills but with the same day-to-day expenses as everyone else, plus a few things extra, because of my disability, the system seemed unwilling or unable to give a little extra, to enable me to have the same quality of life as any other person but just being able to live was good enough for me.

It was a few days later that the postman delivered a large, brown, paper envelope post marked London and with Zandra being the only person I knew from there, I ripped it open to see its contents and was surprised. Inside was a Christmas card from Zandra, a short note and a half a dozen photographs of her posing naked. For the first time I could see the attraction she held to other men but having seen her naked for real in my home, I could get no thrill out of them. In her short letter she informed me that a colleague and friend of hers had been curious about me, she told her that we had been together a fair bit without having any sex and could she bring her friend to meet me. On the bottom of the page was a phone number with a day and time to ring.

Two days later, on the first of December at eight pm, I called the number that Zandra had written on her letter and soon found it to be hers. After talking as two friends do, she informed me that the next day she was flying to Athens for a photo shoot but would be back in time for Christmas and hoped that she would be allowed to see me again on her return. She also expressed a great regret at not being able to see me over the forthcoming weekend, as we had agreed on only a few days earlier, going on to let me know how she had not mentioned to her friend anything about me being disabled. After wishing each other a Happy Christmas I rang off, wheeled into my lounge and asked myself why I did and did not want to see her again but an answer eluded me.

It had been a whole year since I had first met Katherine and nine months since we parted company but I had missed her, although during the weeks since getting my Trike and meeting Zandra, I had thought less of Katherine and more of her, something that surprised even me but that was about to get awkward the day after Boxing Day. At eight o'clock in the morning I was woken by my doorbell ringing and after struggling to get out of bed, I wrapped a dressing gown around me and wheeled to the front door, to find out who it was.

"I don't have to work again until January the fifth and I was hoping you've missed me as much as I've missed you and will let me stay here until I have to go back. Can I? Please?" came the first of several surprises in store for me over the next ten days. Before I could say yes, I remembered something that Zandra had said whilst the two of us were having our meal, in that she was looking to buy herself a place back in London because the tenancy on her current place was due to expire on the 23rd of the month. With warning signals flashing in my head, as well as the sentimental ones in my heart, I was able to compromise and taking hold of her hand said, "I'll be honest with you here and tell you that to have you stay with me for ten whole days would be lovely but I can remember what you told me about your tenancy running out, so I'm asking myself whether you're just going to use me until you've got another place. So the situation is this. I would like it very much if you stayed a while but only for the ten days before you return to work and you'll just have to wait and see how it goes because at any time, if I say go, you must go." Her reply was, to be honest and to a certain extent, a surprise even to me, "I can understand your doubts about me, everyone always does because I'm a nude model who stars in porn movies and as such, people automatically think that I sleep around and use everyone, but that's not true, the work I do is just that a job and nothing more. You've helped me to see that I'm better than what everyone else says I am and you make me feel special and I want to prove to you I can be a lady and love you as a lady should love a man." Hearing this revelation brought a lump to the back of my throat and with the warning signals subsiding but still there, I told her that I was willing to give her staying over a try but she must understand that in no way was I thinking of anything more permanent, which was straight away accepted.

For the next two days Zandra could not do enough for me as she tried and tried to persuade me that I should let her stay the whole ten days, which I started to find too excessive almost to the point of being annoying. Eventually in the evening three days later, I got her to sit down and I said to her, "Don't get me wrong but your non-stop efforts to please me are doing my head in. There's no need to do everything, just be like you were when we first met. How can I treat you like a lady if you are acting like a servant?" I cannot be sure but I do believe she had a tear in her eye over what I had said to her, so I pulled her onto my lap and kissed her. For the first time I could feel a certain amount of affection from Zandra in response to my kiss but suddenly she pulled back from me saying, "I've got a confession to make to you but I'm afraid you'll hate me for it and that would be horrible."

Telling her to just say whatever it was, as I valued honesty even if it was bad, so she paused a second before opening up and telling me. "Remember when I first contacted you and asked to meet. Well the truth is, I was paid to bed you and have sex, by my agent who wanted to use the idea of someone in a wheelchair for a porn film because he said it would be a good laugh. I freely went along with it, that is, until I first met you and was captivated by your personality. I was only paid on our first meeting but every time since, has been because, thanks to you I was able to see myself the way that others do. More than that because you've never even tried it on with me I've fallen for you. Please don't hate me." "Well we'll talk more about that later but first what are you doing for New Year's Eve because it's only the day after tomorrow?" was my reply to her. That night Zandra slept on the couch, letting me have the comfort of my own bed which, to a small degree made me feel guilty, as I had rolled off the couch and onto the floor several times already.

After two nights of sleeping on my couch I decided that night, New Year's Eve, Zandra would have a bed to sleep in and we would both have to face a test, as I would also be in the bed but I would keep it secret until later, after our night out together. As it happened, Zandra herself had a surprise lined up for me, to be given on the stroke of midnight. Going out at ten pm, dressed in jeans, denim shirt and a leather, flying jacket and Zandra in a tight, figure hugging, thigh-length, red dress, black stockings and a pair of red, stiletto shoes, we were soon joining the crowds of other revellers partying in the town centre. As the church bells from all around chimed 12 o'clock, everybody seemed to grab the nearest person and kiss before we all started singing Auld Lang Syne and with that, Zandra reached into her shoulder bag and pulled out a ring, giving it to me saying, "This is for you, the first man to treat me like a lady and the one I'm in love with." Looking at this solid gold ring with 21 diamonds in, I had a real feeling of pride in me and suggested we go home where we could share the bed together, to which, without the slightest hesitation, she grabbed the back of my wheelchair and started pushing me home again, as fast as she could.

That night as I lay in my bed with Zandra in my arms, I felt as I had done that night a year before with Katherine and I could feel a certain fear, that if we made love, very soon she would be gone out of my life, never to be seen again. The following morning, I was woken by Zandra holding a tray, with two fried breakfasts and two glasses of champagne, saying, "This is one way for me to say thank you for not molesting me last night, you really are a gentleman with me." After sitting up and letting her climb back into bed beside me I took a sip of the drink and asked, "You said, one way of saying thanks, is there another?" "I'll show you when we're finished eating this." A slight pause then, "I've actually wanted to thank you that way for ages but I've been afraid to try."

We quickly finished off our meal and Zandra returned the tray with the empty plates to the kitchen before returning to me, removing her night shirt and panties and sliding down under the bedding where I was and started to rub herself against me, whispering, "This is my other way of saying thank you." in my ear and very quickly we were making love. Being the first of January I remember thinking how much I wished the rest of the year would be like this and for several months it was just like that, apart that is, from her modelling jobs abroad.

I can still remember Valentine's Day, when a card arrived from America where Zandra was working, inside of which was a letter asking if I would mind her model friend Jolene, Joe for short, who was currently here in England, visiting me. I did not mind but I did ask myself why, something that I very soon found out. It was a week later that I received a telephone call from Joe, asking to see me the next day because there was something that she needed to talk to me about concerning Zandra. I automatically said OK, expecting her to be the bearer of bad news for me but it was not, as I found out the next day.

Joe called me on her mobile phone mid-morning from the train station, to get direction on how to get to my place, to which I told her to stay there and wait for a disabled man on a Trike to collect her and within the hour I had met her and taken her home to my place. She as expected was a very attractive woman with shoulder length Auburn hair and a shape to as they say die for.

After making us a coffee we retired to the lounge where Joe started to talk, telling me the news. "Zandra has given up making porn movies and is only doing topless modelling since meeting you but that's not the half of it." Stopping to light a cigarette, she continued with, "She is afraid to tell you this because she thinks you'll tell her to get lost but she is pregnant. It's yours." On hearing that I could have been knocked down with a feather, if I wasn't already sitting in my wheelchair. "Why hasn't she told me herself, that's fantastic news." I said, right before Joe gave me the bad news in that because of pressure from her family, who disapproved of their beautiful daughter going out with a disabled guy in the first place, she had gone to an abortion clinic while in LA and had a termination. To hear that was more than I could take and I burst down into tears right there in front of Joe, who tried her utmost to console me. Before leaving I gave Joe a message to pass onto Zandra, in that as far as I was concerned, I did not want to be involved with someone controlled by a family who lived by such old fashioned values and not to even think of contacting me until she had grown up. Before leaving, Joe suggested that she come and see me again because as a parent herself, she felt for me at that time.

Over the following weeks and months Joe became a regular visitor to my place, often bringing her 4-year-old daughter Emma with her, who took an instant liking to me and began calling me her Uncle Mike. Many times during the summer months I could be found with Joe and Emma feeding the ducks that could be found on the small lake in the local park. I found that playing with Emma reminded me of my own daughter Kelly, who would have been about the same age as her if she had not died and also what I could have been doing with Zandra, if she had not had an abortion. Although Joe herself was an unmarried mother and took a strange liking to me, we did not go any further than just being good friends until the arrival of a letter from Zandra in early September, begging to see me.

I remember the day well as it was the Friday morning before I planned to drive my Trike about 150 miles to a weekend show, to help the Disabled Bikers Charity raise some money. It appeared that Joe, had kept in regular contact with Zandra and knowing where I would be on that weekend, she wrote me a letter begging me to see her for a talk, if she got to the show and let her explain what had happened. I made absolutely no attempt to reply to Zandras letter but I was soon to find out that that would not stop her from seeing me.

I finally arrived at the venue in the county of Cornwall about 6.30pm, after getting lost twice getting there on the Friday evening, very tired after having driven such a long way during the day, thankfully in nice weather. I quickly found somewhere to sleep, a tent supplied by a married couple who were involved with the same charity as I was.

On the Saturday morning I awoke in time to see the sun rising above the distant hills with a bright yellow glair, which enabled me to investigate the surroundings that I would be spending the next two days in. A large field a couple hundred yards down a dirt track was basically all it was but by eight o'clock it was being set up with tents, a marquee, stands and to enable the public to see, an arena where the organisers hoped to display some vintage vehicles in the afternoon. When the show got under way at 9am the hoped for crowds never materialised and apart from a few show faithful and a reporter from the local radio station, the whole event was turning into a disaster.

With nothing to do I was very surprised to see Zandra come out from behind a stall and walk right up to me with the reporter from the radio, introducing him to me. Seeing her there before me, I was at a loss as to what to do but the reporter soon grabbed my attention by asking me questions, to go out on the radio later that day. I gave a quick interview to the reporter and without thinking, offered to give a ride around the arena on my Trike during the afternoon of the next day, to anyone who made a contribution to the charity. As soon as I had finished with the reporter, I turned my wheelchair and rolled away from everyone.

Zandra seeing me try to escape from her came after me showing her great determination and grabbing the back of my wheelchair saying, "Don't turn away from me Mike I need to see you and explain. Please don't send me away without giving me the chance to talk to you and explain everything." Feeling the hurt, I had felt over her before, I tried to ignore what she said and keep going but before I could get far I heard her cry out, "Don't go. I'm in love with you." and that was enough to stop me dead in my tracks. Glancing back in her direction, over my shoulder, I saw her burst into a run to catch up with me. Looking up at her and seeing the tears rolling down her face I said, "I'm here until tomorrow afternoon so you've got until then to talk to me. After that I'm going home alone." For the rest of the day we sat and talked, only occasionally interrupted by an inquisitive member of the public, asking questions about my Trike.

Zandra poured out her hard luck story to me, knowing exactly which button to push to get me, so I would become putty in her hands again. You know, the way that only females can do. By that night I had agreed to give her a second chance, something that I never do as a general rule but all the same this time I did but trying hard to be tough, I did put down one condition, that she slept in my tent with me that night, which surprisingly she accepted without question and that night in the cool air of Autumn we made love as if we had never been parted.

The following morning before things got going, I told Zandra that I had promised to get little Emma a present, so the two of us went shopping, looking on every stall in my search and eventually choosing an eighteen-inch-high cuddly dog, which was being sold on a stall raising money for a local kennel. We finished our looking around just in time to get back to my Trike and find a crowd of school children who, having heard my radio interview, had managed to persuade some of their parents to bringing them along in the hope of getting a ride. By noon I was driving my Trike around the main arena, giving rides while Zandra and a charity representative collected donations. Because of the long drive home again Zandra and I said our goodbyes, then parted company mid-afternoon but not before I had forgiven her for earlier in the year and given her permission to see me again. A big mistake on my part as I would soon enough find out.

Chapter 6

I reached home cold and tired very late after over-heating my engine and having to waste considerable time in a lay-by waiting for it to cool down again. I struggled onto my bed and fell asleep still in my clothes, only to be woken by Joe a few hours later calling on my telephone. I told her about my weekend and the gift that I had brought back for Emma before telling her about Zandra's presence there, which she already knew about as Zandra herself had called to tell her the news. Before hanging up the phone, Joe asked if it would be OK for her to bring Emma around the next day because she was driving her crazy with Uncle Mike this and Uncle Mike that, so I said yes.

The lunchtime on the next day being Tuesday, I heard the unmistakable sound of Joe's five door hatchback car pulling up outside and Emma calling through my letterbox for Uncle Mike, so before opening the door to them I carefully hid the cuddly dog behind the armchair in the corner of the lounge. While Emma went searching for the present she knew that she had, Joe and I were able to talk about the weekend's events. I told her how I doubted that I could trust Zandra anymore because of what had happened before and then Joe said something that put my mind at ease. She said, "I know what Zandra done was really horrible to you but her family are a very high status people and are afraid of anything which may affect their standing within the social circle that they live in. Zandras own family only know that she is a model but they think it's a foreign fashion thing and know nothing of her soft porn stuff. It's the shame that her family would feel is why she did what she did and it's been tearing her apart, hurting you as she did because she loves you so much. I can easily see why she loves you as much as she does, as well." Joe's statement embarrassed me a little but not as much as what followed. Putting her arms around me, Joe kissed me passionately on the lips saying, "To be honest with you, Emma wants you to be her daddy and I can see that you would be a great father and partner." Joe's comments were a great compliment to me but she truly had chosen the wrong time to say that to me.

I did not know what to say or do but help was at hand in Emma of all people, when from out of the corner came a cry of excitement as she discovered her present. "Uncle Mike! You're the greatest Uncle in all the world." and then running straight into my arms added, "I love you lots and lots and lots. Thank you." This by itself was not that much help but her next statement put Joe straight, whilst putting myself at ease when she asked, "Are you and Aunty Zandra going to get married now and have a baby for me to play with?" Seeing a little apprehension in Joe's face, I turned to her saying, "I don't know. Should we get married?" Even I could see from her face, that my getting married to Zandra was not what she would prefer, so I added, "No-one will want me as I am now. I'm like a broken toy." After a considerable lecture on how there was nothing wrong with me and that I could easily find a woman who loved me, Joe taking Emma with her, left.

Three days later on Friday I received a call from Zandra, informing me that when she finished work at noon she wanted to travel from London where she was, to see me and hopefully spend her time with me until returning to work. Thinking it was just Saturday and Sunday I said yes but when she arrived in the evening, I discovered that she was not due to return to work for another two weeks. On top of that she dropped another bombshell while we lay in bed that night, by saying, "I'm going to be living at Joe's for a while so I can see more of you." When I asked why she had chosen to live at Joe's, the answer she gave shocked me. She told me that Joe had already expressed having feelings for me and wanting to have sex with me, to which Zandra would not mind, as long as she was there as well. This news upset me deeply, so I told her that she had better go again come morning, as I felt like I was being used as the star of one of their porn movies and being a cripple did not mean that my ethics and morals had ceased to exist.

After considerable creeping and apologies Zandra left early on Saturday, leaving me feeling very hurt, used and insulted. For the second time Zandra had, in a way, betrayed and degraded me and that was one more time than she was entitled to. It was not until Joe came calling on Sunday evening that I did something very wrong and totally out of character for me. Joe came right out with how Zandra was really upset that I had told her to leave so suddenly and asked why. The hurt that I felt over Zandra's comments on the Friday night had made me so angry, that I spoke without thinking clearly when I said, "Zandra thinks you want to have sex with me and wants to join in." Before I could finish Joe butted in by saying, "Yes I do." I continued with, "Come on then. You want sex with me get your clothes off now and we'll do it here and now."

That morning I did something that will haunt me until the day I die, not just having sex with Joe but Zandra, who had been in her car outside, as well. I know that to have sex with two women at the same time is in every man's fantasy's but to actually do it made me so sick afterwards, that it brought about a big flare up in my illness, one that took six months to overcome.

After that fateful day I did not see Zandra again until the following spring, when she returned to this country from America where she was then living, to ask me to bite the bullet and move to the States, marry her and start a family with her. Obviously I refused her offer, preferring to stay in the country where I was born, besides my life was going through some major changes by then and I was still sort of involved with Joe, purely as good friends although we were often more intimate than that.

By this stage in my life it was becoming abundantly clear that a loving relationship with a wife and children was no more than a pipe dreams for me, owing largely to my illness but casual physical short term relationships, be they rare, were just about possible, provided I did not mind being used by the female in question.

Going into 1998, I was becoming quite frustrated with hearing news of breakthroughs in the treatment of my illness, only for nothing to become available to the patients who suffer from MS. For several years I had been speaking to specialists, doctors, social workers and other sufferers who were talking off the record, all suggested the use of Cannabis as a way of alleviating the symptoms of the condition.

Because I had heard the same thing so many times in the past and was well aware of it being illegal to use, I always ignored the talk that I was hearing, until I spoke to a medical person who I trusted outright because of their honesty with me.

After hearing of the discovery of the cause of my condition and it being a genetic one, I think that all suffers become hopeful of either a cure, or effective drug to use, I paid a visit to my medical friend. Because they were very much in touch with the current scientific and medical research, I was hoping to get at least some good out of the visit but I was very soon very disappointed. My friend was able to confirm the discovery, which bucked me up, putting a smile onto my face but that was soon wiped away by the news that, although the researchers had made the discovery they were not using the information to develop a cure or drug but were only interested in developing new ways of diagnosing the same condition. He had heard that the Multi-National drug companies were making too much profit from their existing symptom easing drug sales, which the shareholders valued above the health of the sick. I left my friend very disheartened by the news that I had just received and made a choice, going on what I had just heard and the advice I had already got from all over, about Cannabis.

Because I did not trust the dealers to buy some on the black market, I talked to a good friend who was growing some for his mother, who also suffered with MS and he gave me some seeds of my own to grow. I did grow my own in the conservatory, which was adjacent to the rear of my home and out of sight of everyone. As I was breaking the law by doing this, I as good as shut myself away for five months, until the seeds which I was growing, had developed into plants big enough to use.

Already using legal drugs that carried some side effects, worse than the symptom they were treating, I decided to start using the cannabis as scientifically as a non-scientist could do. Keeping both written and film records of how much, how used and how often used, I began my personal experiment at the start of May. Within only an hour of my first smoke, I stopped using all the prescribed drugs, as the cannabis was doing the job that it was intended for, with not one single side effect and by September I was able to stand up out of my wheelchair, be it by holding on to something but all the same, nothing else had had that effect. By the Christmas I was actually able to take a few small steps using a walking frame as well as walk using crutches at least 200 meters and I could feel my legs again for the first time in several years but as always something messed things up for me.

Chapter 7

It was during early December that a teenage girl had got friendly with me, when I was in the local town doing my shopping after running into me. After the treatment that I had been getting from women in general, either using me to get for what they could get or just basically treating me like I had the plague or something, this young girl was more mature than almost every female that I knew. Because she herself had just been put through a very bad situation, we found ourselves having an awful lot in common and I admit that I enjoyed meeting her in town and getting a burger and coffee so she ate something while we talked, which quickly became a regular thing. One thing that did mean a lot was the way that other females expected me to pay every time but this one insisted on paying her share whenever possible. Something quite rare among the females that I knew.

I can remember one day in particular when, whilst in the town with a couple of friends, soon after first getting to know Suzie, we bumped into her and she quickly joined us. At that time, I did not even know her age so my friends and I tried to guess it. One of my friends in his twenties guessed her age to be about 25 or 35, the other in his early twenties guessed it to be 21 or 22 and I myself guessed it to be 18 or 19 and we were all wrong. It transpired that this sweet, young girl that I had developed a liking for was only 13 years old and subsequently it was wrong to continue being a close friend to her, be it never being even close to sexual and always in public.

Distancing myself proved to be harder than expected, firstly because I had given her my phone number a couple of weeks earlier and she called me regularly and because every time that she was in town, she looked for me. To be honest although I avoided going anywhere that Suzie might be, on the occasions that I was or had no choice but to be, I subconsciously found myself looking out for her and to a certain extent hoping to see her, just to have a person to talk without being made to feel like a freak. She and I had a good friendship until certain people started to spread rumours around, accusing me of being sexual with her which was an out and out lie but when a rumour like that starts, it expands and things naturally become nasty as they did for me.

It all started when a friend of Suzie's became jealous of her because it seems that she herself had a crush on me but I suspect, it was not on me but on the idea of having a boyfriend who had a Trike. I can only blame myself for it all because on one Saturday whilst in the town, Suzie brought a friend up introducing her and after considerable bad behaviour by her friend she turned and said to her, "If you don't stop acting like a stupid bitch I'm going to snog Mike." Suzie's friend expanded on that to start behaving even worse talking very sexually 4xpeisit to us, so she, having had enough, leant over kissing me and stupidly on my part, I responded by kissing her back quickly. That was enough for her friend to start telling her friends that I'd had sex with Suzie which she told me that had wanted to do since first seeing me.

Once the rumours started travelling around the school yard, each child on hearing it added a little bit more, until the parents on hearing it, spread stories around accusing me of being a child molesting, pervert paedophile and that really turned things bad for me and soon enough trouble came knocking on my door. The first I heard of all this gossip was the day that Suzie ran away from home, telephoning me in a really distraught state, crying for me to help her because she had no-one else to turn to that she could trust. This was at 9.30am on a Sunday morning and fearing for her well-being, I straight away got onto my Trike and drove through the rain for a mile to where I found her cold, wet and still crying

After comforting her I suggested taking her back to my place, where not only could she get dry and have a hot drink but also from where I could get onto the telephone and get her some professional help but, on seeing her eight years older 21-year-old boyfriend she went off with him to who knows where. I returned home to have two police officers come calling on me later in the day, having been told that she was with me. Inviting the police officers in they informed me that she had run away from home and they had been informed that she was with me. The two officers, one a six-foot-tall hard looking man and the other a shorter, slim woman asked me what I knew of the situation, to which I related everything that had happened that morning and offering to let them look around my place, just to make sure that she wasn't there before they passed the information back to the station through their radio sets and left, thanking me for my help.

Later that night one of the officers called me to let me know firstly, that Suzie was found safe and well and secondly, that they had heard the rumours and she had confirmed that there was no substance to them. With that news, knowing that I had been proven innocent of the things that I had no knowledge of, helped me to relax and not worry about this lovely young girl, which to me, was welcome. Although things were settled and over and don done with Suzie with as far as I was concerned but, to others they were not, as I was to find out very soon.

It was the second Saturday of October when, just coming out of a shop in town after doing some shopping, that a friend of Suzie's boyfriend, who I had never before seen, walked up to me and slashed me across my chest with a modeller's knife saying, "That's for screwing my mates bit." before turning and running away again. Shocked and scared I went straight to my Trike, drove home and shut myself away. I could not believe that a fit, healthy guy in his early twenties, would show how big and tough he was by attacking a disabled person in a wheelchair, who could not defend himself. I was so shaken up that once I had calmed down, with several strong drinks, I paid attention to the wound on my chest and just like in the movie Rambo, I got a needle and thread and proceeded to stitch it up myself not advisable.

Not going outside of my home until the week after, I prayed that everything was over and forgotten but I was very much mistaken about that and 12 days into November 1999 it happened again. This time a man about 5 feet 8 inches tall with a stocky build and looking as if he had just finished a hard day's work on a building site, came calling at my door. On answering the door, he asked, in a polite calm manner and quite innocently, if I was Mike as he wanted to talk to me, I invited him inside, a big mistake because as I led him inside he stabbed me through the back of my wheelchair saying, "Sick bastards like you deserve to die." and again like the last attack he too turned and quickly left, leaving me with a hole in my back which was leaking blood all over the place. This time, the injury which luckily for me was not as bad as it could have been so easily, was not because at the exact moment that the knife was penetrating the rear of my wheelchair, I had started to lean forwards, hence putting a gap between the wheelchair and my back. Just as before I tried to stitch myself up but this time the needle that I was using punctured a major actuary in my back making things much worse. All the same, I still had to spend most of the night in hospital, where the doctors connected a drip into my arm giving me blood, as I had lost about four pints of my own and would surely have died if I had not called an ambulance when I did. On being returned home again from the hospital in the early hours, I was greeted by more police officers wishing me to make a statement about the attack.

Fearing for Suzie's state of mind, I told the officers that I had fallen over whilst trying to stand and hit something sharp, causing the injury. That would have been OK but for one thing, being the fact that, whilst I was in the hospital my wheelchair was still at home and the police had found the hole in the back of it where the knife had penetrated.

Yet again I found myself being the target of other people's gossip and down and out nastiness, all because I was concerned about the effect that talking could have on a lovely sweet girl, during an already difficult time in her life. The memory of how people who did not even know me, had as good as found me guilty. Those who did know me stopped visiting and turned away from me, just showing me that those I considered friends were actually no such thing. For the next two weeks, police officers went around knocking on every door, sometimes several times to start with, in an attempt to find who had stabbed me but because of the stories being told to them by people who did not even know me, they soon passed on that and moved onto finding proof of me being a child molester. Something that although I was cleared of, I still have bad dreams about and am always fearful of talking to anyone that I do not know well.

My one cancellation in all this was the police turning to me for help to keep Suzie away from her older boyfriend who as well as sexually abusing her and was using her as a drug mule while knowing her feelings for me said that if by sleeping with her could save her life from any of the criminal drug gangs I should but, I never did do that even after she had asked me to for four more years.

As a result of my being a friend to Suzie, I had found myself being visited on an almost daily basis by at least a dozen other teenagers during the November and December of "98", partly because they wanted a friend to talk to but mostly because with the winter months being cold and wet, they had nowhere to hang out to with their friends. So after having a quiet talk to the local police bobby, who was equally concerned about these young children being out on the streets with nothing other than getting involved in petty crime, supported me in opening my home to them where they could gather in the warmth and dry under the supervision of an adult that they trusted. But, as a result of the attacks on me, the second being in my own home, I made the decision to ban all of these youngsters from coming round. Something agreed with by the police and the social services, who had got themselves involved as well.

I did find it maddening to me when a complaint accusing me of raping 15-year-old girl. In my home which was very quickly proved wrong by the fact that at the time and day involved I was actually thousands of miles across the Atlantic Ocean with a new girlfriend ending a claim before even starting and no action was taken against the young accuser on my request for her sake.

With everything happening in my life during these hard times, one thing did remain constant, that being Suzie, who telephoned me regularly to check on me. These calls were a welcome thing to me at this time, until on one Saturday in mid-January while chatting on the phone with her, she declared an unrestricted love for me which for a youngster tends to mean until a better offer comes along. Although this statement was really sweet of her, it was potentially very awkward as I myself had grown a certain love for her almost parental, the difference being, the fact that I knew the difference between loving someone as a friend and being in love with them, which I was definitely not, but all the same under different circumstances and with a much closer age difference I realised that I could so easily have become with her. I found it quite unsettling how the only female to love me at that time, for me the person, was not bothered by the fact that I was disabled and who judged and respected me by my actions, that was a by a girl that morally, ethically and legally was still a child.

Chapter 8

By this time in my life the positive effects of my own trial of Cannabis had worn off and again I was suffering badly from the symptoms of my illness, which were making my life a living hell, especially as I had chosen not to return to the legally prescribed drugs which had been a complete waste of time using. Even like this, I had begun to be affected in other ways and was questioning more and more the politician's motives for not listening to the scientist's, who were confirming the benefits, the specialists and doctors who were asking to be allowed to prescribe it, the suffers whose only relief from their pain from their medical conditions and the 95% plus, members of the general population who supported its use medically, who were still not allowing the sick to legally try to help themselves and the refusal to admit that a naturally grown drug, which had been used worldwide for more than ten thousand years, could be better than the laboratory made artificial drugs.

I started talking to people off the record, trying to get answers to my many questions and was shocked by the things that I was being told. Things like the international multi-national pharmaceutical companies were bribing and putting financial pressure on the politicians, not to allow its use because that would mean them loosing maybe hundreds of millions in profit yearly. The politicians, not knowing how to profit from its use and the basic cold-hearted prejudice amongst the very leaders whose job was to do what their employers (the voters) wanted. But with a new political party in Government, I was able to put my faith and trust in them to listen to the voters and do the right thing. Unfortunately, my faith in our new Government was soon destroyed by their policies and seemingly power hungry actions internationally.

All through this there was only one female that continued to stay in touch and openly admitted to loving me but I still had to keep myself distant from her because it was Suzie, who was still legally only a child. I remember one occasion that I saw her and took her for a burger and cola, where after expressing her feelings for me again said, "It's not fair, I love you and I know that you love me but because of what happened before, we can't go out together blaming her ex-boyfriend not her age. That was where my problem was, still being a child she interpreted my almost fatherly feelings for her as romantic adult loving ones. I don't want anyone to hurt you because of me." Hearing her say this meant a lot to me, as all the other females that I knew were interested in only themselves, but she cared about me and my well-being. It was like a breath of fresh air to me knowing a female that not only liked but appeared to love me, as I was. I can still remember asking myself why this girl could not be ten or fifteen years older but she wasn't and I could never reveal it to her or anyone else.

Even being as lonely as I was, not having a woman to share my life with, I was not desperate enough to do anything bad and stupid with a young girl, like I had been accused of a few months earlier but just as then, people soon started to accuse me of things again. This time, because I had been proven completely innocent of molesting young girls, I was accused of dealing in drugs which I grew in the attic of my home, using the teenagers who frequented my place as dealers and getting under-tens to start smoking, all of which I was 100% innocent of. Being confined to a wheelchair, it was impossible for me to climb through an eighteen-inch square hole about ten feet above my head and very quickly it became apparent that I was being blamed for other people's wrong doings and failure to be responsible parents, something well known around my home. I remember an occasion when the mother and her partner of one child, had a go at me because their child was getting into trouble,and blaming me for it even though I had not seen him for weeks and told me to relocate myself to a different place, saying that others were talking of killing me. Because of this I banned anyone under the age of twenty-one from coming anywhere near me, or my home, unless prior arrangements had been made with their parents and I. I also refused to move away, as to me it would be like admitting to the things I was being accused of. It hurt bad the way that fit and healthy people were targeting their angers and frustrations at a disabled person, rather than admit to their own mistakes and short-comings.

All this was happening during the early summer of 1999, whilst around me everybody was getting excited about the coming millennium celebrations there I was, afraid to go out in case I was attacked again, or being killed before the year was out. My illness had already destroyed my life as a normal person and now other people's hatred was destroying what was left, so much so, that again I started questioning why I should continue living in a world that hated of anything that was different from the norm. Help came for me at this time from an unexpected source, in the form of the three young children of one of my home-helpers. Knowing that I loved looking after children, especially the under-tens and I was good at it, Tracey, being stuck for help with finding a child minder for during the school holidays, asked me if I would mind looking after hers to which I, without hesitation, agreed to doing.

It was in the late May before the schools took a week off that Tracey brought her children to my place one morning for a few hours, to see if firstly, they would like me and secondly, if I would be able to cope with them. Within only a few minutes of their arrival all three of the children took a liking to me, as I did to them. I told Tracey with her tied back straight black hair later that day how they were all polite, very well behaved and basically a pleasure to look after, so after that Tracey found herself constantly being asked when they could go to Mike's again just as Joe 's daughter Emma had. With the school summer holidays coming up, from the end of July to the beginning of September, I found a good reason to snap out of my negative self-pity and get on with my life again, something made harder by other people's unrelenting efforts at causing trouble for me.

Apart from the local troubles around me, other parts of my life were picking up, especially over the Internet. One young lady called Diane that I was in contact with from Canada, was coming to this country on a two week touring holiday and asked me if I would mind her paying me a visit for a day, to which I was happy to do. In mid-June, a knock on the door announced her visit and straight away we were talking as though we had been friends for years. She arrived about 10.30 in the morning and Diane who had not eaten since breakfast the day before was hungry, after an hour of talking told me, so getting onto my Trike I drove us to a public house, where I treated her to a cooked meal while we talked more about ourselves. One thing that I quickly became aware of was how she talked directly at me, not even noticing the wheelchair which I was sat in. The two of us seemed to be getting on so well that I wondered if Diane could be the lady that Kelly had been thinking of all those weeks ago, when she said that I would meet my ideal woman on the Internet during one of many dreams about her.

It was not long before I had a visit from the police, who rightly were investigating complaints being made to them about me. Just as over the previous Christmas period, I insisted that they searched my home for the drugs and pornography that I was being accused of giving to the children and again their search turned up not one single thing. I confirmed to the police officers that I had, on hearing of these accusations, banned all people under the age of twenty-one from coming to my home, which they agreed with. They were also able to confirm my own thoughts and feelings about the attitudes of the trouble making adults who were picking on me, for the simple reason that being disabled made it easier to blame me than admit they were wrong.

On top of that, the Government who had made such great promises when elected was not delivering, where the disabled were concerned. It seemed as though we had been pushed to one side, numbered and ignored. The annual increase to the benefit paid to us, in no way covered the increases to the basic cost of living, which in turn reduced the amount that I had spare to pay my regular monthly bills. I was actually financially worse off than in 1998, the year before. This routine continued for at least the first four years of their power.

With no visitors other than Tracey's three children, I found myself able to face and sort out my own problems. These were the debts that I had accumulated, by spending what money I did have on the local kids and repairing the extensive damages caused by a couple of the troublesome teenagers, that when bored, liked to break things that did not belong to them.

Over the following weeks my only contact with people was mostly limited to my home help visitors, for one hour on two days of the week, Rob, who visited now and then, the occasional bumping into Suzie whilst in the town and the time chatting to people over the Internet on my computer. Whilst talking to people over the Internet, I was able to feel like a normal person instead of, the wheelchair with a senseless cripple in, as the attitudes a lot of society made me feel. Just as Kelly had told me in my dream some weeks before, I was finding myself talking regularly to a lot of women when on the Internet, some of whom began talking about meeting. That was, until I admitted to being disabled, to which they were soon gone again, all except for one lady from Santiago in Chile, who quickly became a good friend to me.

Chapter 9

Katrina is a few years younger than I, divorced like I am, with two sisters whom I also spoke with and a personality that seem to transcend across the ocean dividing our countries and right into my computer, bringing rays of happiness into my heart. It is hard to explain how, or even why but I found myself falling in love with her as if under a spell, even though we had never even met or seen each other. Over the period of three weeks I was finding myself praying for her to be on-line, so that I could talk with her, as I found her to be so very easy to talk to and even after I confessed to her about my disability, she still stayed in touch with me. And then the night came which totally sealed her place in my heart. Or so it felt, for a short period in my life.

It was late one night and I had stayed up just to talk to her, she told me something that made me want to be able to hold and comfort her but the Atlantic Ocean stood in the way, so after asking her for a number, I picked up my telephone and called her. We spoke that first time for a good hour, which in doing so, made me feel like she was right there beside me. I could feel my heart soaking up the emotion and warmth in her voice, so much so that my body began aching to hold and hug her and to let her know that I was there for her. I am not sure but I think similar feelings were going through Katrina at the same time as they were going through me and I knew that here was a real lady who I could quite happily spend the rest of my life with but should I tell her this?

No, was the obvious answer for so many reasons, I had to bottle up my true feelings and keep myself purely as a friend, at least for the time being for all concerned. Fortunately for me, the third Saturday in October turned out to be a good day in several ways. In mid-afternoon I saw the son of the couple who had threatened me a week or so earlier and he told me that his mother had found out that the bad things she had heard about me were lies and was going to visit me to apologise. It never happened.

Whilst talking to Katrina's sister, Angie, the night before on the Internet, I admitted to her my feelings for Katrina, asking her to promise not to tell her of my revelation, as I did not feel that I could deserve her but she told me to confess my feelings because she had a feeling that we would be a very good match and because she had a sneaking feeling that Katrina herself, had feelings towards me. I had intended to keep my feelings secret for a short while at least but when talking to her later on Saturday night, without intending to, I let my feeling be known to her.

Sunday morning came and as I regularly did, I switched on my computer to check any E-mail's that may have been sent to me overnight and received a pleasant surprise. I had one from Katrina, and a picture of her. Now I could put a face to the voice on the phone and the words typed on my computer screen. She was very attractive and even in the pictures, her warmth shone through like rays of sunshine, on which my heart filled with a feeling of contentment and I could not wait to meet her in person, as I considered her to be the most ideal lady for me. It seemed that Kelly had been right in what she had told me about finding a good, loving woman on the Internet but all the same, subconsciously I doubted anything would transpire from our screen relationship and I tried not to get too hopeful and paid more attention to the coming six weeks, looking after Tracey's three wonderful children. Another thing that put uncertainty in my mind was just like Diane, Katrina also came from another country and I was nervous of being used again.

On the day before the start of the school holidays, a Wednesday, I had to travel into the town to do something and was very quickly found by Suzie and a couple of other girls. One of them a twenty-one-year-old called Rachel, who had seen me before and knew that I was an understanding person to talk to, offered to buy me a drink (coffee) if we could get away from the others, to which I agreed to.

Rachel was five feet and four inches tall, with short, straight, black hair and with hazel coloured eyes and looked very much a tomboy, whilst at the same time appearing to be very fragile. Unlike all of the other girls that I knew she did not smoke, take drugs and was still a virgin, choosing to save herself for the right man. This I admired and respected a lot, as well as the way she paid for our drinks, rather than expecting me to pay for whatever she wanted. It did not take us long to relate to each other's circumstances and we quickly found ourselves making plans to see each other again as friends only as she had heard much of the stories made up about me, exchanging telephone numbers but with the start of six weeks' school holidays and having to look after Tracy's three children, seeing much of each other would be hard to do, plus keeping in touch with my internet love.

On the very first day of the school holidays I was up by 7.30am, to get ready for my first day of child minding and at 8.45 the kids came running into my opened back door, all excited at the prospect of staying with me whilst mum and dad were at work, something which I admit went both ways.

Two of Tracy's children, both girls, were in the same age group as Kelly would have been if she had lived and I felt that they would have been friends together, making me feel happy inside. Thinking back now I can't help but wonder if Spending time minding young kids was in a way filling a gap inside because Kelly was no longer there. They were getting so excited about me looking after them during the holidays, that on the Tuesday before the holidays started, Tracey brought them around after school for about half an hour and I could see their excitement for myself. I was touched by what I saw and the coming six weeks with what I had agreed to do, was confirmed as being worthwhile.

The first day started with the kids kissing their mum goodbye whilst I dug out a suitable video to play for them to watch, after which I talked to Tracey about what time she would be collecting them and what I could do during the day with them. Being a warm, sunny day the girls wanted to go to the small park only and play, only a minute's walk from my front door. While the girls went to the park, Tracy's son, David went calling on a friend of his who lived a few houses away from me. With David safely playing with his friend, I wheeled myself up the short path to where the girls, Laura and Susan, were happily playing so as to be able to keep an eye on them. Watching the girls playing together so happy and innocent, I could not help but envisage them playing with Kelly, had she been there, as friends. After all the trouble that I had been put through by others during the previous six months plus, I truly felt proud and honoured that Tracey had the faith and trust in me to look after her treasures.

Everything seemed to be getting much better for me, Tracey was trusting me to look after her children, the teenagers had stopped knocking on my door and were keeping away, I was seeing Suzie less and less and I was getting on better and better with Rachel, plus Katrina was seeming more desperate to meet me in person rather than chat on the phone and Internet.

For the first time in years I was finding myself torn between two women, both of which I had developed a strange kind of love for. I can say that as I know from experience, as a wheelchair with a cripple in, I am not recognised as being a man by a large percentage of women understandably but that to one side, I was getting loving feelings for two women. Admittedly one being from a country on the other side of the world and the other a 21-year-old, who was thirteen years my junior. I was well aware of the big hole that existed in my life by not having a woman to share it with but with the previous year's life that I had been through, I was in a way glad that I was alone and now that things were starting to improve for me, I was not ready for a commitment yet and knew it, so for the time being, friendships were all I was interested in.

For the rest of that week, my days where kept busy with looking after the children every morning and most afternoons, which I enjoyed as much as the kids as well as the afternoons doing jobs around the house and shopping. It was only at night time, that for a couple of hours that I was able to switch onto the Internet and chat with Katrina. On a Wednesday and Thursday afternoon whilst in the town shopping, I did bump into and spend a couple of hours with Rachel, which I enjoyed immensely. All that happened was, we would firstly finish my shopping and then we would go to a cafe for a drink, to enable us to talk more. It was on the Thursday that, without even thinking first, I invited her to go to my place one day for a coffee and chat, which she accepted saying, "I can't today because I have to catch the bus home soon but next Wednesday I'm not working, so I can spend the whole day with you." This should have been a warning to me, especially as it was only earlier that week she had admitted to still being a virgin and was saving herself for the right guy. On top of that she also knew Suzie, who had told her over and over again what a great guy I was but I was only thinking of her as a friend and not a lover or potential wife which if healthy may be different.

On the Saturday morning, not having to look after the kids I was up and in the town by 8.30am, with the intention of doing my banking, getting some petrol for my Trike, having my hair cut and returning home no later than noon but I was quickly side tracked by Suzie wanting a friend to talk to, the friend being me. Just like so many times in the past, she was turning to me with her problems and as always, I took her to the same café as we always did for a coffee so we could talk. It soon transpired that she had had visits from the police on three separate days during the week, relating to other teenagers her age and alcohol abuse. She empathised how she herself did not drink but I know from past experience that she did indulge in drinking but not often, nor in excess like her friends did. As it happened, I ended up spending most of the day with her and several other teenagers, mostly girls, before I could finally get away and go home again.

Getting home again with all my jobs finished, the first thing I did was to turn on the kettle and make myself a drink because being with Suzie for most of the day, I had only had one drink and was dry mouthed and thirsty. I had stayed out for far too long and being a very hot day I was weakened physically by the heat. This I think, was one of the effects of my medical condition, or a side effect from the drugs which I was taking again, now that I had got rid of the Cannabis which was the only drug which helped, without giving bad side effects.

It was not until Sunday evening, after a long hot day of avoiding going out and suffering the loss of strength and use of my hands from the heat, that I received an unexpected telephone call from Zandra of all people, asking if she could visit. Her modelling work was bringing her back to England from LA, in America, where she was now living and she said, "I obviously couldn't blame you if you say no to me because I realise now that I was cruel in the way I was to you. I would like to see you again and try to make amends for what I did. it knows that I can never get you back as my boyfriend but it would mean an awful lot to me if we could try and be friends again." Carrying on, she told me how Joe had kept her informed of my life and the hell that I had been through over the previous Christmas and New Year because of other's actions and the way that her daughter Emma, had been so upset because I had told her mum not to bring her to my place because of the troubles going on. I told Zandra that I needed to think about it for a few days because I was looking after Tracey's kids and they had to come first. Before hanging up she told me that she was not due to come over until early in September and would call again before that, to which I agreed.

I had already chosen not to get involved with Zandra again but the possibility of being just friends with her was a different matter altogether, as I had enjoyed our many nights out dining. And there were other reasons why I could not let myself get back together with her, like Katrina, who was planning on coming over to England to meet me as she was claiming to have fallen for me over the Internet. Then there was Rachel, who was getting friendlier and lived only about four miles away. But more importantly, there were Tracey's three lovely kids who I loved looking after, as much as they loved me looking after them. On top of all that there was Suzie, who appeared to need me to be there to help her cope with her screwed up life because I was the only person that she could turn to in her troubles and trusted.

Going into the second week of the school holidays, I was able to suggest a few ideas with Tracey about what I was hoping to do with her kids while I was looking after them. The first thing being to take them on my Trike to a park situated about a mile away, where there was a small lake with swans, ducks and other water foul. I already knew that she trusted me having them on my Trike but she was concerned about the other road users. I was able to put her mind at ease about that and on the Monday morning we went off for a couple of hours to the park.

As I drove my Trike into the car park near the park, I could feel the electrifying excitement from the seat behind me and I felt a certain fulfilment in myself at being able to give the kids something more than just a TV to watch. Once parked up, the kids jumped off of my Trike and grabbed the bag of bread pieces, which I had put into the carrying basket on the back, for feeding the birds, whilst I unloaded my wheelchair from its position beside my driving seat and transferred myself into it. Walking the ten meters or so to the lake, Tracey's kids very quickly noticed an ice cream kiosk, asking if it was possible for them to have one but due to me having no money on my person I had to decline their request. Although I could not buy them an ice cream they were not bothered by it because I had already brought them to feed the birds at the lake.

For a full hour the kids played and fed the birds, until they had used up all of the bread pieces which we had taken with us, before going into the play area where there were swings, a roundabout, a slide and a climbing frame. Watching them playing so joyfully, I remembered the way, when at their age, I used to do the same things and I was happy inside, completely forgetting all of the troubles that affected my life. Looking at my watch I saw it was just afternoon and knowing that Tracey was due at my place at 12.30, I called to the kids saying, "Do you three want to have an ice cream coz I've got some in my freezer for when we get back!" In less than two minutes we were back in the car park getting ourselves ready to return home. We arrived back to my place just as Tracey pulled up in her car and the kids went straight to their mother, telling her all about the fun they had feeding the birds, before Tracey herself had even managed to get out of her car.

Once back inside the kids carried on telling their mother about the fun they had with me on the Trike and at the park, asking her to let me take them out again. As I went to the freezer to get us all an ice cream the kids continued to relate their morning's activities to their mum who thanked me for taking good care of her children. For me this was like a confirmation of my abilities at being a good and responsible adult, unlike the opinions of others still bent on blaming me for things I was innocent of.

It was decided that during the holidays I would be allowed to take the kids out more but other situations would have to be faced and dealt with along the way. The first of these being Rachel, who was getting friendlier and friendlier toward me, Suzie who seemed to need my friendship more than anything and who could forget Katrina with her getting more intent on coming over to meet me in person.

Just as arranged on the Wednesday of the following week, Rachel turned up on my doorstep and was met by one of Tracey's kids who called me from outside saying, "Mike! There's a girl here to see you." Before I had even a chance to ask who it was the lounge door opened and in came Rachel, holding the hand of one of Tracey's daughters. I had been so preoccupied the previous week that I had completely forgotten about her visit. Knowing that I was looking after young children, she had come prepared with a large bottle of fizzy drink and a big bag of sweets. With that she was accepted straight away by the kids but I was concerned by what Tracey would think of someone else being there.

Being well aware of this I took advantage of the sunshine outside by getting everyone out into my back garden where we played together in the sun until Tracey came to collect the kids at one pm. When she did arrive she told me that she had no complaint with Rachel being there as we had both been giving the children our full attention with no questionable behaviour. And besides, the kids had taken to her and had enjoyed playing tag around my back garden with her. I think that having heard me talking about the kids, she had brought some burgers and bread cakes with her because the kids loved me doing a barbecue and with Tracey's help that was exactly what we did.

For the rest of the summer Rachel and I developed a closer friendship against the gossip that inevitably started, as soon as it got around that I was getting visits from a single woman. I remember the way that Rachel and Tracey were laughing at these stories especially the ones suggesting that I was Tracey's lover. Even Tracey's husband, Andrew heard the stories and laughed along with us as he trusted me not even to think of coming on to his wife which I would never do as I could plainly see the love that the two of them held for each other in their faces every time that they were together. That was something quite all too rare and special.

In a way it was fortunate that no-one knew of my connection to Katrina as yet. We were quietly chatting away to each other over the Internet and by telephone, quite secretly at night times until on Saturday the first of August,2000 when out of the blue she informed me that she had come into some money and wanted to come over to meet me as soon as possible. I was touched by this statement and in a way hoping to meet her soon but subconsciously I doubted that I that I ever would.

It was still about week until the end of the school holidays, which meant that I would be busy looking after Susan, Laura and David a lot, which to me was perfectly fine as I loved having them around. On top of that Rachel was wanting to see more of me which I did not mind, as we had become friends and as for Suzie, she was busy going through boyfriends but still needed me whenever she was upset, and needing for a comforting ear and shoulder to cry on, which I was glad to do but my mind was filled constantly with thoughts of Katrina and the deep love that I believed I had grown for With the country going through a mini heat wave, I purchased a small inflatable paddling pool to put in my back garden, for the kids to splash around in. I had to watch over them playing in the pool from inside, as I could only go outside into the heat for a few minutes at a time before the heat had me becoming unable to use a single muscle, due to the effects of my illness. Something that, only the use of cannabis had been able to stop back in 1998, while I was carrying out my own trial. The pool was an instant hit with the girls who did not want to get out of, even when their mum came for them. To see such young children having fun like they were, made me wish that I could keep them with me all of the year but that would have to stay just a nice thought. It soon became a regular routine with the kids to take them out in the mornings, before the heat started to weaken me and then return back home and play in the pool until mum came to collect them, with us having an almost weekly barbecue, when Rachel came around on one day a week.

With the end of the holidays looming up fast on us, I started feeling a little sad at the thought of not having the kids around each day once they returned to school and so I had a quiet talk with Tracey and Andrew, to arrange one last excursion with the kids before the end of the holidays. Without the kids knowing, it we arranged to take them to the local Burger Bar and have a little party for them. You can imagine the looks on their faces when, on the last Saturday of the holidays, we took all three children to McDonald's for eats. I do not think I have ever seen such happiness or appreciation on young children's faces before. Seeing this, along with the trust and friendship shown in me by both Tracey and Andrew, helped immeasurably in rebuilding my self-esteem and trust in others after the hell that I was put through less than a year before and for that I shall be forever grateful.

With the holidays over and the children gone back to school, I was settling myself to a quiet life until I received two telephone calls that put me into a muddle. The first came from Zandra, informing me that she would be getting back to England a week later and would like very much, if she could, pay me a visit as a friend and the other came from Katrina, asking if I would like her to come over and stay with me, so that we could get to know each other more personally. To Zandra I said, "I don't mind you visiting but there is no way that I want you staying with me." to which she agreed and to Katrina I said, "Just the thought of actually meeting you is more than I could want, so yes, I'll be honoured if you come to visit me." Before hanging up she told me that she had fallen in love with me and hoped that I would not be disappointed with her when we met. How many times have I known the same thing before?

A week later Zandra visited, she behaved like a friend and not, as Joe had warned me, like a woman desperate to get back with an ex. She only stayed for a while but nonetheless, we had time to go out for a meal together, as we had done so many times in the past but she never came home with me, or even hinted at doing so. Whilst together we never once spoke about our time together but spoke about the previous year's happenings for both of us. I think I must have bored Zandra with my continuous talk about Tracey's children and all the fun we had during the summer holidays but I could not help but talk about them. By the time that she left me, I think she had got the message that I no longer had any feelings for her and if she had hoped at getting back with me, she could not.

That took care of Zandra, now all I had to concern myself with was the impending visit from Katrina. That could prove difficult. and surreal. We carried on chatting by phone and on the Internet all through September and into October, until one day she told me on the phone that if I still wanted to meet her I could do so in April of the following year, for about three weeks. Obviously I told her that she would be more than welcome to visit as I had been hoping to meet her myself, almost since we first made contact some months before. She, already having my address and telephone number, informed me that as soon as she had her flight details, I could arrange for her to be collected from the airport and brought straight to my place.

Chapter 10

It was at the start of March of the following year that I received an e-mail from Katrina informing me of all of her flight details and as I had told her, I straight away picked up the phone and arranged the transport for when she arrived. When the day did arrive the 16th April 2000, after a long soak in the bath, I shaved and made myself smell nice before getting dressed in suitable attire for greeting a lady who had just flown from Chile to England, just to meet me. I was feeling special and I must admit apprehensive. What if she did not like me and worse still what if she did and fell in love?

Past experience had shown me that every time something good happened in my life, someone or something always managed to spoil it for me. Up until then I had believed that I was destined to spend my entire life alone and used by others for their own agendas. Even the Government, who I was taught to believe, were there to look after the citizens who voted them into power but even they, refused to let sick people like myself make the choice to use the one drug effective against the symptoms of my medical condition, despite the calls from scientists, specialists, doctor's history and the sufferers themselves. I had become very disillusioned with the nation's policies on the whole over the years but there I was, about to be visited by a woman knowing fully everything about me, who said that she loved me for who I was again I was being given false hope of real love.

At about 10.30pm on Sunday the 16th April 2000 as I watched out of my window, I saw a car pulling up outside of my home and out of it came a young lady. It was Katrina and as I wheeled myself, as fast as I could to open the front door, my heart was filled with excitement at the thought that after being so long in waiting for her, she had finally arrived. Carrying two large suit cases she introduced herself in almost perfect English and I knew by looking into her eyes, that before me stood a young lady even more beautiful than the one whose pictures I had already seen.

I led her into my lounge and almost straight away we started talking about how much we had wanted to meet the other. I was so happy to think that here was a lady whose love for me had brought her half way around the world, leaving her family and friends, her way of life, her culture and her language, just to meet and stay for three weeks, with me.

With it being so late and after the large amount of time spent travelling, I showed Katrina to the only bedroom and told her to get some sleep, as I would stay in the lounge and sleep on the couch that night but she insisted that I sleep beside her that night, so hesitantly I joined her in what was soon to become our bed. Even though it was the last thing on my mind, that night inevitably, we were soon making love in a way that, until then, I had never experienced in my life. That love making continued for several hours until finally, she could no longer continue without some sleep.

The following morning, I awoke feeling that I had been taken to paradise by this beautiful young lady, lying still asleep at my side and I knew that if I was ever to find the perfect person to spend the rest of my life with, I had to do everything and anything to show her that she was it. The good, after so many years of pain, hurt and suffering that until then been my life, can only describe my existence correctly.

By the time that Katrina opened her eyes on her first morning with me I had slid myself out of the bed, gone into the kitchen and started cooking breakfast. Just as I was preparing to serve it, she walked sheepishly in, coming straight over to me and gave me a such a soft, tender kiss. Wanting to treat her right, I told her to go back to bed and I would bring breakfast to her soon, which she did. When I re-joined her she sat and ate the meal, before hugging and kissing me leading obviously to a full day of making love. This, more or less, continued for about three weeks, up until the time that she was expected to leave again. But things certainly never turned out the way that we had expected them to.

She told me that she had been given a six-month's visa for staying in this country and that is just what happened. It made me feel so happy just to be with her and as God is my witness, my love for her grew stronger every day. In my heart everything was perfect but in my mind I felt that once she left, I would never see her again. This was due mostly to several problems that appeared because of my illness. Several times I found myself crying inside because something had happened to me medically and I could plainly see the frustration in the eyes of her, at not being able to do anything to help me.

All though for the six months that she was here with me, she brought me happiness, giving my life a true meaning and to me the incentive to keep fighting against both my illness and the prejudicial action of both the government's rules and society in general. I could not help but feel also, that in some way or other she was only using me. Her words always said the right thing to me but too many times her actions, or lack of them, were affecting my ability to fully trust her, even when I saw her snogging the guy who was supposed to be my friend, so I knew, but kept it to myself so she never knew what I had seen until after she had departed for good.

Even after she departed from my home to return to her home country, I found myself being told by almost everybody that she had met, that she had no intention of ever coming back and was making plans to chase after other men. I tried my utmost hardest to ignore these things and think of them as just other examples of societies determination to stop any possibility of my ever having a life as a human being but when I received two telephone calls from overseas, one from America and the other from her own country, telling me the same thing, I could not continue ignoring it any more.

Before leaving, I had promised to send Katrina the money to cover the cost of her plane ticket when she went home and because I have never broken a promise in my life that is just what I did, even though it was done at the expense of my living on a diet of only one loaf of bread per week, so I could not only save the money to send to her but also, to pay all the built-up bills that I had avoided paying whilst she was here, to give her everything she needed and a lot of what she wanted.

Katrina left my home on the 12th of October 2000 and it took me until the April of 2001 to get my finances straightened out and send her all of the money that I had promised to send. This was made so much harder by the English Government who, despite saying that they would be increasing the benefit to the severely disabled, something that I was classified as, an extra £35 plus, a week in the December of 1999, I was still not getting any of it, instead as with the previous two or three years, I was even worse off financially, often forcing me to live on bread alone for several weeks at a time. After that I made myself a promise to never open myself up to a woman again, until one proved to me through her actions, that I would not find myself being hurt and betrayed again.

That was until the autumn of 2001 when, just as with Katrina, I invited a lady from Canada over for a visit, which unlike before turned out a failure, admittedly equally on my part. Barbara, unlike Katrina, only stayed for two weeks and did bring her own money with her. Surprisingly to me, she informed me that she had been working in a specialist MS unit for 23 years and very quickly told me that some of the symptoms that I suffered from were not MS ones. She also invited me to visit Canada, where she wanted me to meet her father, who was a very well respected specialist doctor there. So come the early June I was on a plane flying overseas, something that I had always wanted to do. For two weeks I felt like a tourist seeing the local sights, taking lots of photographs and generally being happy.

After my two weeks stay with Barbara I returned home with things to keep me busy. The first, being the promise of a visit by Barbara over Christmas and the knowledge that both she and her father, both of whom had plenty of experience with MS sufferers, doubted my diagnosis. This started me thinking about my health since 1987, when I was told how I had one of five things, the least serious of which was MS so that was what they would call it. Just before Christmas, as arranged, she arrived to spend the festive time of year and left again early in the January of 2002. I wanted to keep in touch with her but my internet access was cut off, along with my telephone and having moved house, I had no address for her, so there ended yet another chapter in my life. I will always remember her with fondest memories for giving me the incentive to live my life rather than to just exist.

Chapter 11

With that part of my life over, I soon found myself back where I had been before, in my rented bungalow, sitting alone at my computer chatting to complete strangers, for hours on end. I was getting to be almost a recluse, like I had been before, when on one night I found myself talking with a lady who was not only in as difficult a position as myself, but only lived about 300 miles away from me.

I had been on the same contact programme for the whole day, with only a limited number of people wanting to converse, mainly about the weather where they were and the latest movie etc. You know, the sort of thing that bores the heck out of you. I had just about given up for the day and was about to turn my computer off, when for some reason my attention was drawn to a name on my screen and without being fully aware of what my fingers were doing, I typed "Hi, fancy a chat?" Expecting to get no reply like usual, I was answered with "Yeah but it's getting very late here so I can't chat for long." Because of it being very late we only chatted for a few minutes but a few minutes was all that it took to agree to chat again the following day.

The next evening Ann and I were back online as arranged, sharing our stories and getting to know each other before arranging to be online for a chat the following day. We carried on like this for a relatively short time before I cannot remember who did, but one of us hinted at meeting. The next thing I knew, was one Friday in the February of 2002, I was sat in a taxi outside of the town's train station, awaiting the arrival of a coach with Ann on. I already had an old picture of her, so as one coach, followed shortly by another arrived, the cab driver, with the picture, met every woman looking vaguely like her asked, "Are you meeting Mike?" until he was answered with, "I am." Escorted by the cab driver, a very good and respectful man. . Ann got into the cab so that we could go back to my place that I had spent the previous couple of days cleaning, as best as I could. After a weekend of talking and getting to know one another in every way possible, I escorted this wonderful, young lady back to the bus stop so that she could go home again, with no idea that in a year's time, we would be saying, "I do." and I had joined a family that had accepted me as a man rather than another burden who would use and abuse her as unforgivably as her two ex-partners had done to her.

This catching a bus down to Devon from Yorkshire a journey of 300 miles became a weekly trip until we changed the slower bus to a train to have more time together but when Ann let slip that she was starving herself just to pay the cost made me feel so bad that I knew that I had at last found a woman who truly loved me for me.

I guess that Ann is not the sexy model men generally dream of but the beauty within her as a person shot her straight to the top of the list of everything good and precious to me. Yes, without even knowing or wanting it I had joined with a female equivalent of myself.

As we became more and more as one together we grew a greater trust and dare I say it a greater love for each other. Working together with everything especially in rebuilding Ann's self-esteem and her own self-worth after the years of degrading abuse both physical and emotional by her ex-partner. I well remember the feeling of contentment with a love that just grew without even trying after so many failures up until then, I believe more so by my own failures and I am both sorry and glad of it because I am so happy in my life now with the direction that it is going in. Even with the improvident my life Ann on the other hand was deliberately being victimised by the members of the children's section of her social services making totally false accusations and invented lies about her including the social worker that Ann believed was helping her, that is she took me to meet her.

After being introduced to the social worker we handed her a full criminal report on me showing that as well as not having anything illegal or bad against me there was nothing to stop me from being a child minder if I so wished after training, but the worker refused to accept it because they had not had it done themselves. After about thirty minutes of encouraging words we left with Ann more hopeful while I only saw treats In her words and I told Ann not to believe or trust her. Something that was proven true very soon.

It was during the September of 2002 when Ann telephoned me still living in Devon 300 miles away from her in a devastated way after having to go to one of the social services secret court hearings where the true nature of her social worker was revealed in her new set of lies supported by her superior who is just as dishonest. Without any hesitation I told Ann that I get to her as soon as I could which unfortunately was a few days later, but I arranged to stay with Ann for three days to help her to cope with another unjust action by the social

To make things worse for us an internal cyst pod on my coccyx which had burst because I was unable to deal with it as advised by a community nurse for several years already with no problem resulting in my not catching my train home as planned but having to spend the night in Scunthorpe hospital There I started with the Emergency doctor could not tell me what the problem was along with 4 more experts all of whom refused to listen when I told them exactly what it was and how I had been told and had been dealing with it including a man telling me to shut up because he was the top registrar while I was the patient and knew nothing. The following morning after being discharged sitting on a new wheelchair cushion enabling Ann who had managed to get to me to take me home to her place. Having already missed my train home to Devon I told Ann that if she wanted I would stay with her for as long as she wanted which was welcomed by the few people who had met and seemed to have approved with me, with the exception of the social services until they started using the fact that I am disabled against her calling me a danger to her children in my wheelchair and was unable to do anything on my own despite the fact that I was living on my own in a bungalow which I kept good as spotlessly clean without any help. Something that I doubt most social workers would or could do themselves.

What proved confirmed my hatred for social workers in the area where Ann lived was the day that in front of her and under oath in court the claimed to be independent children's rights officer told complete lies against her providing the social the excuse for reducing the little contact with her children. Luckily for us Ann was sent an official letter which was undeniable proof that the children's rights officer was not just helping the social services but also showing her discrimination against disabled people. When confronted by myself and Ann she tried to deny she had even said or wrote it even when faced with the proof of her illegal talk under oath witness by Ann and her solicitor. Unfortunately, under the national laws at the time any true justice was prevented by those in power who had no respect and regard for the for the less wealthy than themselves and guilty themselves of at times worse but I will say a big thank you to the many like that who do genuinely know and are as angry as the rest at the abuses of power for their own selfish wants.

As for me all this was to be the beginning of a new life as the man who is in a wheelchair instead of a wheelchair with a useless good for nothing in and that alone helped my belief in myself. To begin with the specialised wheelchair cushion that Sculthorpe hospital had replaced mine with very quickly clearly showed that the area where the cyst in me had burst was causing a breakdown of my skin resulting in constant need for cleaning and dressing due to bleeding. This also increased the pain that I was already getting used to from my MS. When the officially called pressure sore after having my wheelchair cushion replaced by several different ones with no change became too bad with the stench of rotting flesh I was readmitted to Scunthorpe hospital where I was placed in a single room after one night on a ward following day because of understandably complaints by other patients at the stench being given off by my body. I had not fully known that the called sore on me was actually large enough to fit a clench fist and deep enough to pass my coccyx leaving it hanging unattached. After the usual blood tests plus I found myself with not a reason for my situation as hoped but having myself given concentrated antibiotics by introversive drip for two or three days solid causing my body unable to keep down even a single sip of water let alone food almost killing me.

With the obvious concern by Ann and myself at the hospitals treatment of me by their supposed specialists I demanded being moved back to our local Hospital where after being placed in a private room due to the hospital super bug MRSA. I was given another blood test that showed that I was infected with a flesh eating bacteria hence the size of my wound and the smell of rotting meat. That should have been done at Scunthorpe proving their failure of care. I could only have been infected by the bacteria during my earlier visit to the hospital which understandably makes me wonder if someone knew and was willing to kill me through the treatment received on my second stay to keep a secret but I am thankful for the excellent care given by the ward staff there.

It was now the April of 2003 and I was still in the local hospital but after talking with the specialist I was now under I was allowed to discharge myself for 24 hours so that Ann and I could have our planned wedding in church with all of Ann's children being there and included. This was not particularly what the social services wanted to happen as it would cause them an extra person to hide their crimes from and they knew that not only had I had problems from them in the past and came out better than them but knew almost nothing about my own past. Under normal circumstances this change in Ann's situation may well have altered their victimization of her but alas I believe the risk of sacking or even prison if exposed for what they had been doing for many decades made them even more inventive with their illegal actions.

I honestly believe that if not for the strength of our love for each other and her own family who several male relatives had already been target with untrue accusations by them we may well have not survived to be together as a family.

Author's Gallery Over the Years

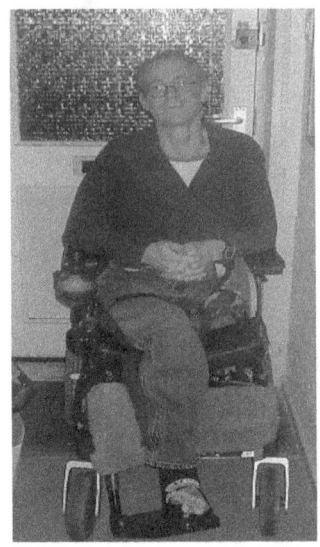

Figure 1. Home after first leg came off

Figure 2. Dressed up for Christmas 2011

Figure 3. Me in 2004

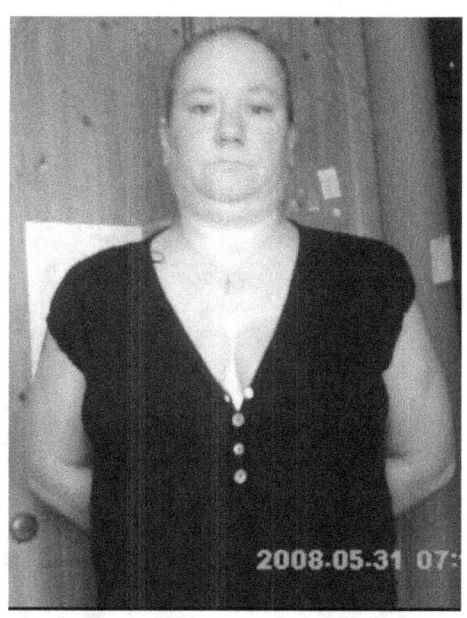

Figure 4. My Lovely Michelle 2007

Figure 5. Me with only one leg

Figure 6. My wife Michelle in 2003

Figure 7. Me posing for picture

Figure 8. My custom-built Trike

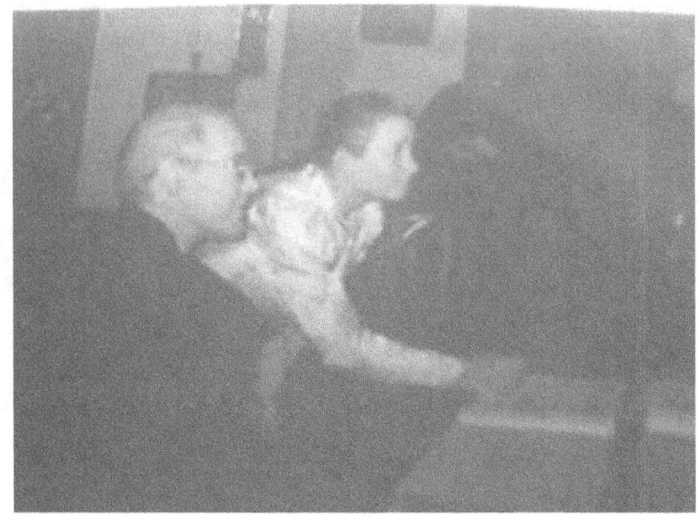

Figure 9. Wedding day in April 2003

Figure 10. After 3 months using cannabis

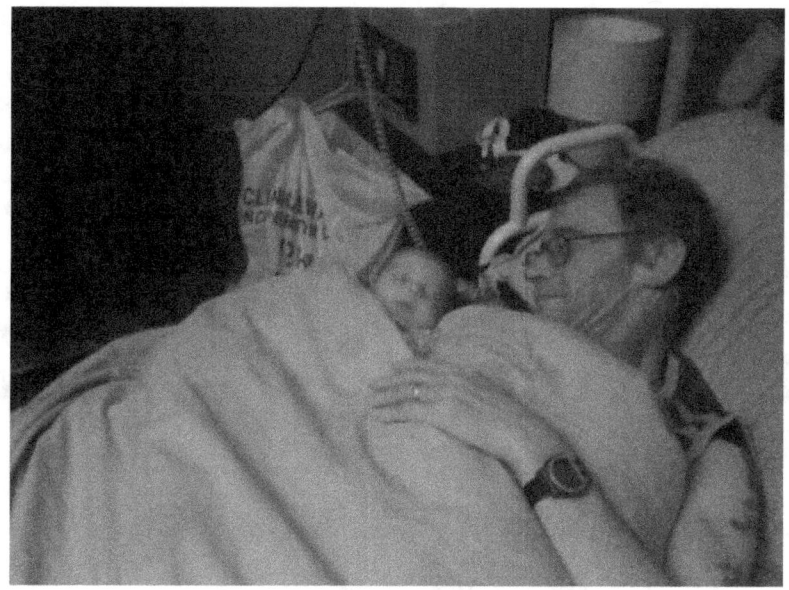

Figure 11. Granddaughter sleeps when grandad is there

Figure 12. Raising money for NABD national association of bikers with disabilities

Figure 13. After 4 months using cannabis

Figure 14. Me in Year 2012 with my Awesome T-shirt Sign

www.ingramcontent.com/pod-product-compliance
Lightning Source LLC
Chambersburg PA
CBHW071507070526
44578CB00001B/468